Capitalism:
the moving target

LEONARD SILK

Solomon

Capitalism:
the moving target

With contributions by Kenneth J. Arrow
Thomas Carvel
John Kenneth Galbraith
Andrew Glyn
Gabriel Kolko
Edwin Kuh
Wassily Leontief
David Rockefeller
Paul A. Samuelson
Gilbert Sorrentino
Paul M. Sweezy
& Studs Terkel
Illustrations by Jean-Claude Suarès

QUADRANGLE
The New York Times Book Co.

Acknowledgment is here made for: On p. 54, excerpt from "The Age of Anxiety" from *Collected Longer Poems* by W. H. Auden, copyright © 1946 by W. H. Auden and reprinted by permission of Random House, Inc.; on p. 55, excerpt from "The Reply" from *Kaddish and Other Poems 1958–1960* by Allen Ginsberg, copyright © 1961 by Allen Ginsberg and reprinted by permission of City Lights Books; on p. 55, excerpt from "Sometime during eternity" from *A Coney Island of the Mind* by Lawrence Ferlinghetti, copyright © 1958 by Lawrence Ferlinghetti and reprinted by permission of New Directions Publishing Corporation and MacGibbon & Kee Ltd.

Library of Congress Catalog Card Number: 73–81188
International Standard Book Number: 0–8129–0396–X

Design by Charlotte Thorp
Production by Planned Production

TO CALVIN BRYCE HOOVER

CONTENTS

PREFACE

Heywood Broun—the greatest columnist of all time, for my money—once explained how he got to be so disrespectful of the capitalist system, unlike Walter Lippmann. At Harvard, he said, "Walter Lippmann and I had been in the same class and had had the same opportunities, only Lippmann attended the lectures of Professor Carver, while I kept cutting classes to watch Tris Speaker play with the Red Sox. If only the Boston outfield had not been so good that year I might understand a lot more about the sanctity of the gold standard . . ."

I myself had the good luck to learn about capitalism not from Thomas Nixon Carver at Harvard in 1909, but from Calvin Bryce Hoover at Duke in 1940. Professor Hoover, though no enemy of the system, has no illusions about it, having been born the son of a poor Illinois farmer and gandy dancer on the railroad. It was Professor Hoover, I think—I have lost my lecture notes—who first referred in my presence to capitalism as a "moving target," so for that reason alone, although there are far more important ones, this book is dedicated to him.

More immediately, this book had its origin as a series of articles for the Op-Ed page of *The New York Times,* and I am most grateful to my *Times* associates, John B. Oakes, Harrison Salisbury, Herbert Mitgang, John Van Doorn, David Schneiderman, Betty Pomerantz, and Jean-Claude Suarès, whose insightful artistry illuminates any subject, for their gracious support and editorial contributions.

The idea of the project was to take fresh soundings on where capitalism is "at this point in time," as the Watergaters have taught us to say, with an effort to get a sense of where it is going —or ought to go. The intention was to assemble a group of contributors who would look at the system from different perspectives—not only from different political or ideological perspectives, but also from different cultural perspectives.

All the pieces in the book except Galbraith's, Sweezy's, and mine first ran in the Op-Ed series on capitalism. John Kenneth Galbraith's essay, which he submitted for the series, was simply too long for the page, even the whole page. Although Mr. Galbraith thought the editors had done a skillful job of trimming it, he preferred to have it printed only in its entirety; it is his presidential address to the American Economic Association, which he delivered in Toronto on December 29, 1972, and I sympathize with his feelings about it. It is a brilliant and limpid piece, strongly and carefully structured, and it would have been painful—to me, if I may say so, as well as to Professor Galbraith—to have left out any of it.

After the Op-Ed series on capitalism had been concluded (at least in the view of its editors), Paul Sweezy, whose name had been taken in vain both by Kenneth Arrow and Paul Samuelson, felt that he deserved a chance to respond to their assertions that, as any competent contemporary economist (such as himself, though a Marxist) knew, the Keynesian revolution in economics had solved the problem of depression and unemployment, so capitalist wars were no longer necessary, at least for the purpose of sustaining full employment. Mr. Sweezy insisted he knew no such thing. I invited him to spell out his rebuttal in this book, and he accepted. The discussion would not have been complete or fair without his response.

My own long piece was written only after we decided to make a book of the series. I have drawn on articles of mine that first appeared in *The New York Times, Economic Systems and Public Policy,* and *The Research Revolution.* This earlier material has been rewritten.

I have gained much knowledge and stimulation from all the contributors to this book and thank them warmly for their essays. I am grateful to my son Mark for really splendid research assistance and good advice.

LEONARD SILK

August, 1973
Montclair, New Jersey

PART ONE

Capitalism:
the moving target

I

Centuries before the system we call "capitalism" acquired a name or a theory, medieval theologians sensed its revolutionary nature and the danger it posed to the social order. As early as the twelfth century the stiffening attitude of the Roman Catholic Church toward usury represented an awareness of the threat of this strange and powerful economic force to the medieval ideal of a harmoniously ordered society.

It was usury—the demand for and the promise of the payment of interest—that brought capital into being and launched capitalism upon its revolutionary career. "No wonder that the guardians of the medieval order of values were up in arms against it," writes the Catholic historian Werner Stark, for here

. . . was the cancerous cell which, if not excised from the body politic by the surgeon's knife, would grow ever more rapidly until it had eaten out the vitals and brought on destruction and death. It has been said more than once that the Doctors did not understand the phenomenon of capital, but that is decidedly less than fair. Certainly, they did not have an express theory of it, but they realized, however dimly, what its true nature is—to be the spring of economic change and advancement, to be the motor force of progress. Here again the contrast between medieval and modern conceptions becomes strikingly obvious. We think economic progress desirable, whatever the cost; they counted the cost and found it excessive. Only Almighty God can say who is the wise man and who is the fool in this business.[1]

Whether for good or evil, the passion for growth is the essence of capitalism. In the United States, growth—founded on technological progress—became virtually a national religion. The "booster spirit" acquired a quasi-moral force of its own, transcending other moral values.

II

During its relatively brief history the United States has had successive great waves of economic growth, each lasting a little more than half a century. The first, based on cotton textiles, iron, and steam power, lasted from the end of the American Revolution until the eighteen-forties. The second, based on railroads and steel, lasted until the end of the eighteen-nineties. The third, based on electricity, the automobile, and oil, lasted until about the middle of the twentieth century. The fourth and current surge of growth got under way during World War II. It is based, not on a few technological innovations, but on a host of them, stemming from scientific progress in nuclear and solid-state physics, organic and inorganic chemistry, electronics, engineering, the earth sciences, the biological sciences, and mathematics.

[1] W. Stark, *The Contained Economy: An Interpretation of Medieval Economic Thought* (*The Papers of the Aquinas Society of London*, No. 26. London, 1956. Reprinted in Leonard Silk, ed., *The Evolution of Capitalism*. New York, 1972), pp. 18–19.

What will this new epoch be called? It is clearly an understatement to call it the atomic age, as we did at the end of the war. It is too narrow to call it the age of automation. It is more than the space age. What we are passing through might be called the Scientific Revolution or perhaps the Research Revolution, a more sophisticated and profound outgrowth of the Industrial Revolution.

Doubtless the most important factor in launching this new revolution, in which basic science has emerged as the initiator of industrial, social, and political change, was the success of organized research on military problems in World War II. Early in the war British scientists moved into high positions in their government and industry to attack a wide variety of problems. After the United States entered the war, the Office of Scientific Research and Development performed the same function and initiated many of the wonders crucial to Allied victory. The most dramatic and significant of all was, of course, the Manhattan Project, which enlisted the talents of many scientists and engineers in the search for the atom bomb. In the chemical industry there was urgent need to find a way to synthetically replace natural rubber; again, the search was successful. The war also brought forth radar, antibiotics, and the first giant electronic computers. The old Marxist-Leninist thesis was that capitalism needed war for the imperialist exploitation of new geographical areas or to maintain prosperity at home. A newer thesis might be that capitalism needs war to justify massive expenditures on science and technological development.

But the research revolution deepened and widened after the war. It yielded sensational innovations, such as "peaceful" nuclear reactors, new generations of electronic computers, jet aviation transports, atomic ships and submarines, communications satellites, and spaceships. It also yielded hosts of more prosaic but fast-growing innovations, such as titanium sponge, polyethylene, argon, styrene plastics, resins, and antibiotics. And it brought forth a mass of small electronic gear: television sets, radios, desk and hand calculators, hearing aids, tape recorders, cassettes, telephone attachments, electronic bugs.

III

The transistor provides a striking illustration of the way science powers economic growth in the new research revolution.

The search for the discovery of the transistor was a race against time to remove the greatest single impediment to the continuing growth of the Bell Telephone System. By the mid-nineteen-forties that system was expanding not only in size but complexity—outgrowing the limits of components such as relays and electronic devices with conventional vacuum tubes. By switching from manual to automatic exchanges in the thirties and forties the telephone companies had solved a labor and cost problem by eliminating central operators, but they now required more and more skilled maintenance crews to keep the system operating. What was needed was a new kind of switch, one that would not wear out and that could be produced at reasonable cost.

The first step toward that goal, though no one realized it at the time, was taken early in 1940 in the office of Mervin J. Kelly, then president of Bell Laboratories. Russell S. Ohl, a staff member working with silicon metal (one of the most common semiconductor materials), demonstrated an unusual photoelectric cell made from pure silicon. Until that time photocells had operated on the electrical effect produced by the interaction of the surfaces of two different metals exposed to light. Ohl's cell generated current in a single piece of metal; and the current was about ten times stronger than usual.

One of the witnesses at the demonstration was Walter H. Brattain. Sixteen years later he and two fellow physicists, William O. Shockley and John Bardeen, received the Nobel Prize for their work with transistors.

It took years to build enough knowledge of semiconductors even to predict a device that could amplify or switch current. The research team at Bell Labs had to break unknown ground in metallurgy and chemical analysis and do some abstruse theorizing in quantum mechanics.

The pieces of the puzzle suddenly fitted together in 1947. In November of that year Bardeen and Brattain produced a low-frequency amplifier by immersing a piece of silicon in a salt solution. In doing so they demonstrated a theory of space charges, propounded by Shockley. The next stride came only a month later, after the team had switched from silicon to germanium, which was another common semiconductor material, but one that was easier to handle. Brattain then noticed the first amplifying, or "transistor," effect in a solid semiconductor. In June 1948 the transistor made its official debut to the Bell Labs staff, the press, and the military.

The first devices were point-contact transistors, so-called because they consisted simply of two sharpened wires pressed into a piece of germanium. In the transistor's passive state almost no current would flow through the germanium between the two pointed wires, but if a tiny current were introduced into the germanium by a third wire, the electrical resistance between the two point contacts would virtually disappear. Then a much larger current could, conceivably, flow between them. That simple

7

phenomenon is the essential magic of electronics: a small current can control a larger one. This process can go on in successive stages, almost as fast as a streak of light, until an original tiny signal has been multiplied millions, even billions, of times and can do dozens of wonderful things, like vibrating the cones of loudspeakers to produce sound, turning on a rocket motor, and changing the direction of a spaceship hundreds of thousands of miles from the earth.

The point-contact transistor was a partial answer to the need for a better switch: it had no parts to wear out or burn out, and it was incredibly small. But electrically and mechanically it was weak and fragile. Its noise limited its use as an amplifier. It could do only a few of the jobs that were easy for vacuum tubes or relays, and this limited its applications. Besides, Bell Labs' physicists didn't really understand why it worked. Until the answer was found, production of the devices was doomed to remain a chancy business; it was doubtful whether high-volume, close-tolerance production was possible at all.

Despite its drawbacks, the point-contact transistor proved that a solid-state amplifier would work. The next advance required more basic research, this time into the properties of crystalline semiconductors and, with the help of mathematical theory, into the behavior of electrons in solids. From these studies Shockley in 1949 was able to predict mathematically that it would be possible to produce a new type of transistor based on a single crystal of semiconductor material (the point-contact transistors were made of material with many crystals). Instead of causing current to flow between two delicate wire points, Shockley proposed a method of controlling current flow between areas of impurity elements in the crystal itself. These impurities introduced into the single crystal would be so tiny that ordinary chemical or metallurgical analysis could not detect them. Because the boundaries, or "junctions," between differing impurity levels would be relatively much bigger than the wire points in a point contact, a junction transistor could handle much more power, Shockley theorized.

Before Shockley's theory could be put to practice, more basic research was needed. Metallurgists and chemists had to find ways of making germanium purer than any material had ever been before. Impurities could make up no more than one part in a million, or several in a billion. It was, said one scientist, "like trying to separate a pinch of salt evenly distributed through a trainload of sugar when you didn't even know the impurity was salt."

Not until 1951 could the first junction transistor be made to work. Even then it seemed doubtful that transistors ever could be built to fit predetermined specifications. But in 1954 Bell Labs again achieved a breakthrough. William G. Pfann, a metallurgist, invented zone refining. This is a high-frequency heating technique that can melt a localized area of a long ingot of germanium or other metal and sweep the melted zone through the length of the ingot. The melted material is either a more or less effective solvent for impurities than the solid; so it sweeps the impurities in the metal to one end or the other of the crystal.

This technique was a boon. It not only purified the germanium but also concentrated the impurities in one end, where more of them could be identified. It also provided a way to spread impurities evenly, under close controls, through the crystal. Thus, with vastly improved materials, the semiconductor industry was born.

When the semiconductor industry began its growing—enormously increasing the growth potential of the entire electronics industry—Bell Labs held basic design and process patents covering the whole field. The growth gained impetus from Bell's policy of putting these patents virtually in the public domain. Western Electric, which handles the licensing arrangement for American Telephone and Telegraph, offered licenses on reasonable terms to interested firms in the United States and foreign countries.

Bell Labs invited scientists and engineers from all over the world to visit its facilities and conducted symposia on significant semiconductor developments. Why was it so generous? Jack Morton, a Bell Labs vice president, said: "There was nothing new about licensing our patents to anyone who wanted them. But it was a departure for us to tell our licensees everything we knew. We realized that if this thing was as big as we thought, we couldn't keep it to ourselves and we couldn't make all the technical contributions. It was to our interest to spread it around. If you cast your bread on the water, sometimes it comes back angel-food cake."

But—and here is a point worth the attention of skeptics about the value of antitrust legislation in the modern industrial society—the antitrust suit initiated by the Justice Department against AT&T in 1949 had a powerful effect in influencing the company's decision to disseminate its new technology. That antitrust suit sought to separate AT&T from Western Electric, its manufacturing arm; an attempt by AT&T to dominate or monopolize the new semiconductor industry could have ruined its defense in the antitrust case.

In 1956 AT&T signed a consent decree ending the suit. This left Western Electric within AT&T but required Western Electric to license all existing patents royalty-free to any interested domestic firm and to license all future patents on reasonable

10

terms. AT&T was allowed to require cross-licensing of patents. This only ratified what had already been done in practice. The semiconductor industry grew rapidly, as technical discoveries were rapidly interchanged either through licensing or through the job mobility of scientists, engineers, and managers.

The result was a rapid growth of the industry and a multiplication of firms.[2] In 1951 the only firms involved in the production of transistors were Western Electric, General Electric, Raytheon, and RCA. In 1952 Bogue Electric, Clevite (later a part of International Telephone and Telegraph), Motorola, and National Union Electric got into the business. In 1953 Texas Instruments, Radio Receptor, Transitron, the Columbia Broadcasting System, Sylvania, Tung-Sol, and Westinghouse started manufacturing transistors; in 1954 came Amperex, Honeywell, Philco-Ford, Thompson Ramo Wooldridge, and General Instrument. Then dozens of new firms followed. It was not just a process by which new firms diffused the original Bell Labs technology; the new firms contributed greatly to the entire industry's pool of technology. New American firms played a crucial role in the rapid electronics revolution because, as John Tilton has shown, their smaller size permitted faster internal communication; allowed a faster response to changing market opportunities; and enabled them to employ the kind of person willing to accept the great risks involved in pioneering the use of new technology, since the new firms could provide "rewards commensurate with the risks."[3]

Whether one likes its fruits (computers and hand-held calculators) or fears them (electronic bugging and data banks full of personal information), the swift rise of the semiconductor in-

---

[2] See John E. Tilton, *International Diffusion of Technology: The Case of Semiconductors* (Washington, 1971).

[3] Tilton, ibid., p. 162.

11

dustry—so crucial to the expansion of the huge electronics industry and to the increasing productivity of the entire industrial process—demonstrates the enduring strength of the capitalist system. Its fantastic ability to keep radically transforming society, creating both material wealth and social disorder, seems, if anything, to be greater than ever. It is, however, in the very nature of successful capitalism to force change in capitalist institutions.

IV

We in the West have learned to pay attention to the periodic outbursts over Communist ideology, such as quarrels between the Stalinists and the Trotskyites in the early nineteen-twenties or between the Maoists and the Khruschevites in the early nineteen-sixties. As abstruse as such debates may sound to those unlettered in Marxism-Leninism, they usually reflect and often foreshadow major historical developments. By comparison, debates among capitalists over their own ideology seem mild and are often dismissed as tiresome semantic or public-relations exercises with little or no significance.

Yet it is becoming apparent that an ideological controversy which in recent years has been agitating the more thoughtful and articulate businessmen and professors of economics and business administration does reflect a central political, economic, and business issue of our time: whether business organizations are going to bind themselves ever more closely to the state, or whether they are going to try to reverse the trend toward a more holistic state by battling to regain greater independence from government control or other "outside" interference.

On the ideological level the debate has taken the form of an argument between proponents of the traditional "free enterprise" creed and the more recent "social responsibilities" creed. The free-enterprise creed holds that the aim of business is and should be to maximize profits, within the legally established rules of the game. In the words of a 1926 disciple of the creed, "It is inconceivable to a one-hundred-percent American that anyone except a nut should give something for nothing."[4]

Put more politely (as it is by liberal economists, in the old-fashioned sense, or libertarian economists, as we say nowadays, like Professor Milton Friedman), the pursuit of self-interest or maximum profits is still, as in Adam Smith's day, the most logical and efficient way to run a business, and the only way to preserve a free society. In Friedman's words:

Few trends could so thoroughly undermine the very foundations of our free society as the acceptance by corporate officials of a social responsibility other than to make as much money for their stockholders as possible. This is a fundamentally subversive doctrine. If businessmen do have a social responsibility other than making maximum profits for stockholders, how are they to know what it is? Can self-selected private individuals decide what the social interest is? Can they decide how great a burden they are justified in placing on themselves or their stockholders to serve that social interest? Is it tolerable that these public functions of taxation, expenditure, and control be exercised by the people who happen at the moment to be in charge of particular enterprises, chosen for those posts by strictly private groups? If businessmen are civil servants rather than the employees of their stockholders, then in a democracy they will, sooner or later, be chosen by the public techniques of election and appointment.

[4] This was the view of William Feather, a publishing executive and regular contributor to *Nation's Business* in the nineteen-twenties; it is quoted in James W. Prothro, *The Dollar Decade* (Baton Rouge, 1954), p. 43.

13

And long before this occurs, their decision-making power will have been taken away from them.[5]

The new social-responsibilities creed, by contrast, holds that this free-enterprise philosophy is an anachronism. Critics of the old creed say that it may have made sense in the days of smaller companies, of something closer to free competition, and of tyrannical kings, but that it makes little sense in today's society, in which large corporations play not only a vital economic role but also an important political and social role. These corporations cannot avoid having a heavy and conspicuous impact on society, which the society, if sufficiently disturbed, will move to curtail or prevent. If business wants to retain its essential autonomy, say proponents of the new business creed, it must be prepared to assume certain social responsibilities and to be sensitive to public attitudes. Thus, according to this view, the businessman must try to coordinate his company's and his own private aims with the public interest.

But skeptics ask: What is the public interest? Is it simply what the President of the United States says it is? Is he to be regarded as infallible, especially when there is no legal obligation to submit to his view? What if some White House aide or lesser official ventures to state the "public interest"? Should the citizen —such as the head of a large corporation or trade union—simply accept this view?

Is it necessarily true, in any case, that the public interest, however defined, is inherently superior to private interests or desires? Must poets or composers give up their work, their private visions, to help clear slums or, more alarmingly, to write odes to slum clearance and, instead of serving the dictates of their consciences,

---

[5] Milton Friedman, *Capitalism and Freedom* (Chicago, 1962), pp. 133–134.

14

serve instead some patriotic purpose? In the economic area, if inefficiency is held to advance the public interest, shall corporations become less efficient? Shall individuals decide what to produce or consume and how much goods and services are worth, or shall the State? But does this correctly pose the issue? Is it rather that powerful heads of business institutions largely control government and themselves define what they call "the public interest"?

There are good grounds for being skeptical about business's altruism. Indeed, American businessmen themselves, like Americans generally, are determined not to appear "do-gooders" or "goo goos." They commonly deny that they ever behave altruistically. In this respect they appear to have changed not at all since the early nineteenth century, when Alexis de Tocqueville observed that "the doctrine of self-interest" found universal acceptance among Americans, who, he thought, often failed to do themselves justice. Even though he found that the Americans, like people everywhere, sometimes give way to "those disinterested and spontaneous impulses that are natural to man," he reported that the Americans seldom would "admit that they yield to emotions of this kind; they are more anxious to do honor to their philosophy than to themselves."[6] A century later American businessmen generally backed the Marshall Plan to rescue a war-devastated Europe, insisting that they were only following enlightened self-interest. Paradoxically, many of the same hard-headed Americans were outraged by the alleged failure of Europeans to be more grateful for America's professedly nonaltruistic behavior. During his tenure as Secretary of the Treasury in the first Nixon administration John B. Connally often found occasion

[6] Alexis de Tocqueville, *Democracy in America,* vol. 2 (New York, 1945), pp. 130–131.

to remind the Europeans of their debt of gratitude to the United States.

Because of Americans' habit of proclaiming their philosophy of self-interest, the nation's critics—including not only Europeans uneasy about United States hegemony and Russians and Chinese trying to maintain or extend their own empires, but also revisionist American historians—find it obvious that American foreign and domestic policies are nothing more than business interests lightly disguised.

Yet, despite their continued espousal of self-interested motives and their celebration of the need for higher profits, more and more American businessmen, especially the leaders of some of the largest corporations, are seriously seeking to come to terms with and to serve national interests that may impinge upon their business interests. Some insist that, whatever the definitional problems, there certainly is such a thing as the public interest and that a good citizen should seek to discover and advance it as best he can. Joseph L. Block, former chairman of the Inland Steel Company, has declared that those individuals who deride the public interest as a "nonexistent will-of-the-wisp, a self-serving device used by politicians to cloak ulterior objectives" are denying not only the need of private parties to consider the public interest but even the right of government to define the public interest. Such views he regarded as "utter nonsense." "Surely," he insisted, "the greater good of the nation as a whole should be of paramount importance to everyone, and while no one has an omniscient power to define 'public interest' accurately at any given time, and certainly not all of the time, it surely behooves all of us—and most particularly government—to endeavor to do so."

The real problem, however, is not to define the public interest in general terms but to define it in relation to specific issues—and then to find the right private or public, or private-cum-public, policies for coping with those issues.

Depending on the particular issue involved, on the mode of the business-government relationship, and on the interests or ideology of the observer, close cooperation between business and government may be regarded as "liberal" and "socially responsible" or as "reactionary," "corrupt," and even "fascist."

V

In recent years both Democratic and Republican presidents have been striving for a new balance in the relationship between the federal government and the business community. A decade ago President Lyndon B. Johnson declared that government and business must "operate in partnership," not as antagonists, to solve many problems, of which, he said, the foremost were the following: accelerating the rate of economic expansion, maintaining price stability, strengthening the United States balance of payments, and "finding ways to reduce the tragically high rate of unemployment among teenagers, and assuring adequate economic opportunities for all our people not now in the mainstream of American prosperity."

In attacking those problems, Mr. Johnson suggested, government and business each had a role to play. Government's responsibility was to produce a tax system that would not overburden businessmen or consumers and would maintain incentives for productive effort; to shape expenditure programs that would improve human and natural resources and make those social investments "needed to support private enterprise"; and to keep a "clear

17

field" for private business in areas where competitive enterprise is the most efficient way of getting a job done. Government must develop fiscal and monetary policies to promote balanced and stable growth and to act "promptly and decisively when the nation is threatened by either recession or inflation."

Business's responsibilities, as defined by President Johnson, included producing "high-quality goods" and "new and improved" items, cutting production costs, and vigorously selling goods both abroad and at home. At the same time business should follow employment policies that would offer workers both job security and incentives to increase their productivity and incomes. Business should plan capital investment programs in ways that would contribute to smooth expansion and should avoid inventory problems which in the past have "often been a source of economic instability."

But Mr. Johnson's definition of business's responsibilities did not stop with such noncontroversial tasks. He urged commercial banks not to raise the interest rates they charged their customers. At that time, late in 1964, the Federal Reserve had, for balance-of-payments reasons, just raised the discount rate, and the President was eager to keep the prime rate charged to domestic business borrowers where it was, for fear of slowing economic expansion. Mr. Johnson said he was sure bankers realized that their own long-term interest was inseparable from the prosperity of the nation and warned that a recession might force the government to increase spending and further unbalance the budget. Mr. Johnson also urged business to respect the "noninflationary wage-price guideposts" that had first been spelled out by President John F. Kennedy's Council of Economic Advisers in 1962. Private business should put forth extra effort to increase its exports; President Johnson later supplemented this plea for help in closing the payments gap with a strong call for "voluntary" programs to curb bank lending and direct investment abroad. He also called for private business to end discrimination against Negroes in employment and to support increased educational and training programs for the poor.

Implicit in all these presidential recommendations and requests was the conviction that the free market does not provide satisfactory answers to many crucial economic and social problems facing the nation. To be sure, free-enterprisers would argue that government continuously undermines the free market and prevents it from doing its work of allocating resources efficiently and facilitating genuinely voluntary solutions to those problems. But champions of the social-responsibilities creed, while expressing their regrets about government interference, nevertheless have little faith that, in a highly industrialized, large-organization system, the market can produce prompt and satisfactory solutions. They prefer to seek workable answers rather than waste time bemoaning the political or economic changes that have kept Adam Smith's "invisible hand" from doing its work.

Whether explicitly or implicitly, enthusiastically or regretfully, that was the line taken by Presidents Roosevelt, Truman, Eisenhower, and Kennedy, besides Johnson. And, nominally, it was the line that President Nixon sought to change—by reducing the social responsibilities, not just of business but of government itself. In his second inaugural address of January 20, 1973, Mr. Nixon declared:

In trusting too much in government, we have asked of it more than it can deliver. This leads only to inflated expectations, to reduced individual effort, and to a disappointment and frustration that erode confidence both in what government can do and in what people can do.

19

Government must learn to take less from people so that people can do more for themselves.

Let us remember that America was built not by government, but by people—not by welfare, but by work—not by shirking responsibility, but by seeking responsibility.

In our own lives, let each of us ask—not just what will government do for me, but what can I do for myself?

But this stern doctrine was meant to apply to welfare clients, not to failing corporations seeking relief. The prime example was the Lockheed Aircraft Corporation. The Nixon administration asked Congress to authorize a $250 million loan guarantee to save Lockheed and its (civilian) L-1011 Tristar airbus program. The bill that the administration sent to Congress did not mention Lockheed directly but only proposed loans for major business enterprises in danger of failing—thereby establishing the general principle of corporate bail-outs, at the discretion of the administration and its congressional supporters.

The Nixon administration also applied the antitrust laws with remarkable discretion. Here the prime example was the International Telephone and Telegraph Corporation. Indeed, what the Great Depression did for the general theory of employment, interest, and money the ITT case may do to advance the theory of industrial organization. The expansion of knowledge in this area should lead to a deeper understanding of how the American political-economic system really operates.

Not long after his appointment as President Nixon's first head of the Antitrust Division, Richard W. McLaren told a Senate subcommittee investigating the problem of conglomerate mergers that the concentration of economic power had been growing dramatically in the United States since World War II. From 1947 to 1968, he said, the two-hundred largest corporations in manufac-

20

turing had increased their share of total assets from 46 per cent to 60 per cent. "In light of these facts," said Mr. McLaren, "I think it would be entirely appropriate for Congress to seek to ascertain what implications a continued rise in economic concentration has for a competitive economy and . . . for our political and social institutions as well."

However, Mr. McLaren said he saw no need for new legislation in the area of conglomerate mergers; he was confident he could stop supersized mergers under the Celler-Kefauver Act and on the basis of earlier Supreme Court rulings.

The Celler-Kefauver amendment to Section 7 of the Clayton Antitrust Act presumed that, when any purchase of one company's stock or assets by another tended to reduce competition substantially or tended toward monopoly in any section of the country or any branch of commerce, divestiture of the stock or assets would be the remedy. And the Supreme Court had firmly laid down the line that economic hardship was no defense for a corporation against divestiture, if needed to break an anticompetitive merger.

In the 1961 Supreme Court majority decision, ordering Du Pont to divest itself of General Motors stock, Associate Justice William J. Brennan, Jr., stated that "if the Court concludes that other measures will not be effective to redress a violation, and that complete divestiture is a necessary element of effective relief, the Government cannot be denied the latter remedy because economic hardship, however severe, may result." Justice Brennan added that this proposition "is deeply rooted in antitrust law and has never been successfully challenged." He cited a string of cases, including the first Du Pont case of 1911, the American Tobacco case of 1911, Corn Products in 1916, and Crown Zellerbach in 1958.

21

Curiously enough, however, the report of the merger of ITT and Hartford Fire Insurance Company, prepared by a young private financial analyst and commissioned by President Nixon's special assistant, Peter Flanigan, was almost entirely concerned with the hardship that would be done to ITT if ordered to divest itself of Hartford Fire's stock.

And the Ramsden report was a key factor that, according to former Assistant Attorney General McLaren, caused him to change his mind about taking the ITT cases to the Supreme Court. Yet, in his February 18, 1970, testimony to the Senate Subcommittee on Antitrust and Monopoly, Mr. McLaren had said the three ITT cases (Canteen Corporation, Grinnell Corporation, and Hartford Fire) plus two others (the Ling-Temco-Vought acquisition of Jones & Laughlin Steel and the proposed Northwest Industries' acquisition of the B. F. Goodrich Company) were his five principal cases for enforcing the antitrust laws.

All five cases, he said, involved "the elimination of potential competition, the creation of power to engage in systematic reciprocity on a large scale, the entrenchment of leading firms in concentrated markets, and the contribution to, and proliferation of, a merger trend."

The economic analysis contained in the Ramsden report of the ITT–Hartford merger must have struck an ardent antitrust lawyer, such as Mr. McLaren, as curious.

Mr. Ramsden noted that the stocks of several large casualty and multiple-line insurance companies had gone up by 60 to 100 per cent from their 1970 lows and offered the judgment that the earnings outlook for the insurance industry was bright, because rates were likely to go up as costs went down. Rates were going to rise, said the Ramsden report, because of the "improved regulatory climate." Some twenty states accounting for over half of all premiums written had adopted open competition or "file and use" rating laws permitting companies to file rate increases immediately, subject to later regulatory reviews. This, said Mr. Ramsden, would permit rates to rise faster than in the past.

At the same time the insurance companies' costs were going down for three reasons: companies had withdrawn or radically reduced "their exposure to unprofitable markets such as high-risk urban areas"; as insurance companies adopted the practice of cancelling insurance policies when claims were filed, policy holders were "becoming increasingly circumspect about the claims they submit to their insurance companies"; and, as inflation subsided, the rate of increase in the cost of claims would subside, while, as federal and state auto safety standards got tougher, the costs to the casualty insurance companies would decline.

Quite apart from the dubious social implications of the report, in its implicit approval of the insurance companies' refusals to insure urban centers and racial ghettoes or of their dissuading policy holders from making legal claims, the Ramsden report obviously assumed that there was so little competition among the insurance companies that declining costs would not mean lower insurance rates, but the opposite.

The bright earnings outlook of Hartford Fire Insurance was only one factor that attracted ITT's roaming eye; its rich liquid assets was another. At the same hearings on conglomerate mergers at which Mr. McLaren had drawn compliments from the chairman, Senator Philip Hart of Michigan, for his crusading zeal, Professor Abraham Briloff of Baruch College, an accounting expert and reformer, emphasized the drive of conglomerate corporations to acquire insurance companies—as Leasco had acquired Reliance Insurance, City Investing had acquired Home

23

Insurance, and National General had won Great American Insurance.

The conglomerates, said Professor Briloff, coveted the insurance companies' "huge pools of liquidity, their cash flow . . . and their latent pools of suppressed profits represented by the unrealized appreciation in the portfolios accumulated by the insurance companies" over a century or more.

There was, he explained, a "symbiotic relationship" between conglomerates and insurance companies.

In the case of ITT and Hartford the symbiosis proved to be more powerful than the earlier antitrust zeal of the Justice Department. When the Watergate case broke, Special Prosecutor Archibald Cox emphasized that the ITT–Hartford merger was joined to the Watergate affair through the large contributions of ITT to the Nixon campaign.

Professor Theodore Lowi has noted that, except for a few martyrs, such as the crusading Assistant Attorney General Thurmond Arnold of the Roosevelt administration, who have sought "vainly to use government to decentralize industry," the net impact of attitudes toward business from conservatives as well as liberals has been to *restrain the competitive system*.[7]

Richard McLaren, who joined the Nixon administration eager to reverse the trend toward industrial concentration, did not achieve martyrdom but left the Antitrust Division to become a federal judge in Chicago, taking the place of Judge Julius Hoffman.

Alas, the political-economic-financial symbiotic forces had been too great. As Professor Lowi sadly concludes, "One might say that the only differences between old-school liberals and conservatives is that the former would destroy the market through public

[7] T. J. Lowi, *The End of Liberalism* (New York, 1969), p. 66.

24

means and the latter through private means."[8] And sometimes the liberals and conservatives join hands.

VI

The difficulties in cracking the nation's outstanding economic, social, and environmental problems are aggravated by our ignorance of how the American political economy really works. We have statistical models—national-income models, input-output models, flow-of-funds models. But none of these is satisfactory in showing where *power*—both political power and economic power—resides in the system. Both kinds of power are involved in shaping the decisions that do so much to determine whether prices go up or hold firm, whether funds flow abroad faster or slower, whether blacks and other minorities find it harder or easier to get particular jobs, whether investment flows to particular regions or not, whether government spending will be increased or decreased (and for which programs), whose taxes will be cut or raised, and so on. Conventional economic theory assumes that all such decisions are made by the market or in heaven.

On the contrary, the American economy has clearly been growing more closely integrated and holistic, and this trend creates the setting in which individuals who head important business or financial institutions may exert greater control over the system. One student of this trend, Father Paul P. Harbrecht, has suggested that the American economy now consists of three different but interlocking systems.[9] The *primary* system, in his view,

[8] Lowi, ibid., p. 66.

[9] Paul P. Harbrecht, S.J., "The Modern Corporation Revisited," *Columbia Law Review* (December, 1964), pp. 1410–1426.

is made up of the network of large manufacturing and service corporations; these finance themselves to a large extent through depreciation allowances and retained earnings and may even provide financing for their own customers. The *secondary* system consists of the markets for corporate stocks and bonds, mortgages, and all other forms of debt instruments. The *tertiary* system includes the financial intermediaries that began as services to business but have so evolved as to permit individuals, including workingmen, to participate more fully in the operations of the primary and secondary systems—through their shares in savings and loan associations, pension funds, mutual funds, life insurance companies, and credit unions.

The capitalist system, says Harbrecht, "seems well on the way to digesting itself." All the financial institutions have been increasing their stockholdings rapidly; they have been spending considerably larger sums of money to purchase equities than all individuals together. In addition, financial institutions now own more than 80 per cent of all outstanding corporate bonds.

The growing interdependence of the major components of the American economy appears to have a "taming" or "civilizing" effect upon corporate executives. Although it may be true that, as Adolph Berle and Gardner Means sought to show, corporation managers are largely free of direct stockholder control, indirect pressures on management are possibly greater than ever.

Corporate officers are extremely eager to see the value of their company's securities appreciate in the market, and not only because they themselves may have significant stock holdings or stock options. In part, corporate executives want to see the value of the company's securities appreciate because this makes everything about their jobs easier: it is easier for them to raise additional capital in the markets, if it is needed; to justify salary increases for themselves; and to launch investment programs, make acquisitions, or start new ventures to increase the growth of their companies. Further, executives often develop an intense loyalty to their corporations that goes beyond simple personal enrichment or power, even though personal and corporate goals are commonly bound up together.

Business executives appear to "internalize" the aims of their institutions, just as do newspapermen, college professors, labor leaders, and preachers. Corporate executives usually suffer mental stress when they see the value of their corporation's securities fall. And they know that this may shake confidence in their ability, not only among stockholders and their own directors, but also among their suppliers, customers, bankers, and financial institutions from whom they might need support. One who works for a large corporation knows full well that when profits are high and rising, life is exhilarating, and nothing is denied the enterprising manager, but that when sales and profits are falling, life grows tense and grim within the corporation, and heads may roll.

The subordination of personal to corporate (or national) interests can be a dangerous and even vicious thing—for the individual, the nation, or the corporation. In considering such cases as B. F. Goodrich's manufacture of an air brake too light for the L-T-V Aerospace Corporation's A7D attack aircraft, Libby McNeill & Libby's marketing of 300,000 cases of cyclamate-sweetened fruit bread after the Food and Drug Administration had banned the cyclamates in the United States, and Dow Chemical's manufacture of napalm for use in Vietnam, Robert L. Heilbroner asserts that such "profiles in corporate irresponsibility" are business atrocities "like My Lai."[10] He contends that, like that slaughter

[10] R. L. Heilbroner, *In the Name of Profit* (New York, 1972).

of South Vietnamese civilians, business atrocities are "not merely hideous exceptions, but, rather, discovered cases of a continuing pattern of misbehavior." Yet he correctly observes that the very persistence of the corporation gives the search for responsibility a deeper significance than the remedy of the abuses of the moment.

For every nation, capitalist or Communist, must have the equivalent of large modern corporations. Technology forces men and machines to be organized into huge productive units; hence, whatever the name of the political-economic system, the creation of a responsive and responsible corporation becomes an indispensable step in the creation of a responsive and responsible state; and this is perhaps the central social problem of our age.

The problem of dehumanization affects all large organizations, whether these are the Nazi S.S., the Communist bureaucracy, armies, air forces, the White House and executive branch of the United States government, or the multinational corporations. The danger is that any large organization, which has objectives of its own that may not accord with broader principles of personal and social morality, has the power so to reward or punish individuals as to undermine and overcome their personal sense of responsibility.

This is not merely a modern but a very ancient human problem. As the French nobleman, the Duc François de La Rochefoucauld said, "We are oftener treacherous through weakness than through calculation."

In an open and democratic society, however, pressures build up on corporations—through the press, through independent public-interest groups, through large investing institutions (including universities and pension funds), and through the con-

28

sumers and voters—to behave more responsibly, whether they like it or not and whether or not it accords with traditional free-enterprise ideology. (The same sort of pressures build up on the national government, producing unpredictable effects, as in the case of the Pentagon Papers, disclosure of which by the press apparently had the effect of driving the Nixon administration into paroxysms of espionage and authoritarian behavior.)

Some corporations, however, are showing a healthy ability to respond to social pressures and criticisms. This does not necessarily please their critics. Ellmore C. Patterson, chairman of the board of the Morgan Guaranty Trust Company, told an audience in Paris that "the younger and more perceptive critics of American business" are close to the mark when they complain, not that businessmen are arch-reactionaries, but that they are refusing to play "their assigned role as stubborn antisocial villain."

But the critics retort that the corporations are only demonstrating another maxim of the cynical La Rochefoucauld: "We often do good that we may do harm with impunity."

VII

What is good and what is harmful, however, is no longer self-evident.

Increasingly, executives of large corporations are coming to see that, if they are to keep their own companies growing, it is essential to keep the entire economy steadily growing. They see that in many important respects their corporate interests are becoming consonant with those of other groups in the system: that is, with the interests of political leaders who are pressed to

29

produce full employment, stable prices, and balance in the nation's international economic relations; with labor leaders, who must try to gain job security and rising real incomes for their unions' rank and file; with other producers, who want the demand for their own products to be high and rising; and with the managers of the banks, life-insurance companies, pension funds, savings-and-loan associations, and other financial institutions, who want to be sure that savings continue to flow to them and that their own investments produce stable and rising returns. In this interdependent system the nation's business leaders begin to see a clearer need to concert their aims with those of other important policymakers, whether in business, banking, government, politics, labor, education, or other institutions.

But it is not easy to trace or understand the linkages, even within the business establishment. This is an old American problem. Half a century ago a congressional committee found that an "inner group" of 180 financial leaders held a chain of 746 directorships in 134 of the nation's largest corporations. In 1913 a subcommittee of the House Committee on Banking and Currency, headed by Representative Arsene P. Pujo, suggested that there was a "money trust" that had come about as the result of an "insidious monopolistic scheme."[11] The Pujo committee declared that it was a "fair deduction" from the testimony that "the most active agents in forwarding and bringing about the concentration of money and credit" through various means, including interlocking directorates and "influence," were J. P. Morgan & Company; the First National Bank of New York; the National City Bank of New York; Lee, Higginson & Company; Kidder, Peabody & Company; and Kuhn, Loeb & Company. To these

[11] *Report of the Committee to Investigate the Concentration of Control of Money and Credit, House Report No. 1593,* 62nd Congress, 1913.

charges J. P. Morgan & Company submitted a reply (which the subcommittee refused to print), declaring:

The testimony failed to establish any concerted policy or harmony of action binding these 180 men together, and as a matter of fact no such policy exists. The absurdity of the assumption of such control becomes more apparent when one considers that on the average these directors represent only one quarter of the memberships of their boards. It is preposterous to suppose that every "interlocking" director has full control in every organization with which he is connected, and that the majority of directors who are not "interlocking" are mere figureheads, subject to the will of a small minority of their boards.[12]

The Morgan reply declared that for a private banker to sit upon a board of directors of some company with which the bank does business "is in most instances a duty, not a privilege." The banks and leading investment houses, it said, were continually being pressed for representatives to serve on the boards of corporations whose securities they handled, and in general they accepted directorships only on those boards "which the opinion of the investing public requires them to enter, as an evidence of good faith that they are willing to have their names publicly associated with the management." There was nothing at all sinister, said J. P. Morgan, about "this natural and eminently desirable relationship."

Today the situation seems little changed. In 1965 another Congressional committee, headed by Representative Emanuel Celler of New York, looked into the issue of corporate interlocks. After examining the boards of 74 of the largest industrial companies, banks, and insurance companies, the staff of the committee cal-

[12] Letter from Messrs. J. P. Morgan & Co. in response to the invitation of the Subcommittee (Hon. A. P. Pujo, Chairman) of the Committee on Banking and Currency of the House of Representatives; Feb. 25, 1913, p. 9.

culated that their 1,206 board members had a total of 4,608 management links with other companies.[13]

Moreover, there was a great deal of interlacing of boards within the group of 74; some 182 businessmen held down a total of 425 directorships in the group. The directors and officers of American Telephone & Telegraph had 104 management ties; those of its manufacturing arm, Western Electric, had 37. The management of Western Electric was connected with 91 other companies; General Electric, with 84. However, the number of links varied greatly from company to company: Bethlehem Steel Corporation had a completely "inside" board, and the oil companies generally seemed to discourage many outside ties.

The Celler committee did not suggest that these corporate links were illegal. The Clayton Antitrust Act bans a sharing of directors only between competitors, but it does not proscribe "vertical relationships," where, for instance, directors of the three major automobile companies may meet together in the board room of the Morgan Guaranty Trust Company. But, while the Celler report conceded that adverse effects of corporate links are not apparent, it stated:

It would be naïve not to think that the ability of two corporations to compete is not impaired by common management members; that individuals who occupy top management positions in corporations that deal with each other will not have their judgments beclouded by considerations that affect their own financial interests; and that an individual who is too busy to appear at the board meetings does not debase the management of the corporations he serves.[14]

[13] *Interlocks in Corporate Management: A Staff Report to the Antitrust Subcommittee of the Committee on the Judiciary, House of Representatives*, 89th Congress, 1st Session, March 12, 1965, p. 230.

[14] *Interlocks in Corporate Management: A Staff Report to the Antitrust Subcommittee of the Committee on the Judiciary, House of Representatives, 89th Congress, 1st Session*, March 12, 1965, p. 230.

The report suggested bringing corporate officers besides directors within the reach of the Clayton Act and extending the prohibition itself to include "vertical" and "indirect" management interlocks. That has not yet been done, but the Federal Trade Commission has begun to move more vigorously against competitive interlocks. In 1973 the FTC accused three corporations—the Aluminum Company of America, Kennecott Copper, and Armco Steel—of having illegal interlocking directorates. The complaint was based on that section of the Clayton Act which states that "no person shall at the same time be a director in any two or more corporations" if they are competitors.

What is new about this FTC action is that it was brought against three companies that would once have been regarded as in separate industries. But the FTC contended that the markets for steel, aluminum, and copper actually overlap. Clearly, steel does compete with aluminum for use in such products as building materials, automobile bumpers, engine blocks, and cans, aluminum competes with copper in tubing, electrical conductors, and heat exchangers, and all three metals compete in household utensils and other uses. The case was resolved when the executives concerned simply resigned from their interlocking directorates.

Slowly the antitrust authorities seem to be broadening the Clayton Act's opposition to corporate interlocks. The danger is that interlocks muffle and suppress competition and give unfair advantage to corporations with inside representation on the boards of other companies. This may give a special edge to banks whose officers often serve, as in J. P. Morgan's day, on customers' boards, to the disadvantage of competing financial institutions not so represented. A more vigorous enforcement of the Clayton Act could bring about a healthy restructuring of relationships among many of the nation's largest corporations, a broadening of the base of corporate control, and a desirable increase in the competitiveness of American business and industry.

Would it be worth the effort? Once again we are up against the classic riddle of whether the modern industrial economy needs more, rather than less, planning and control or stiffer antitrust prosecution and more competition.

Antitrust remains, as the late Richard Hofstadter put it, "one of the faded passions of American reform"; he held that we have moved from the age of *The Curse of Bigness* and *Other People's Money* to that of *The Lonely Crowd* and *The Organization Man*. Still, antitrust holds an important place in the American *mythos*. Liberals can support it because they retain their old suspicion of business behavior, and conservatives because they still believe in competition as a little extra leverage in the battle against inflation.

The broad public seems to accept and even like corporate bigness; in an age of television, mass communications, and *anomie* many people apparently like big corporations, whose names and advertising they can recognize.

Periodically, however, a story breaks—such as the ITT case, complete with Dita Beard and the document-shredding machines —that reawakens public distrust of big-business behavior and regenerates support for antitrust action.

Even business itself accords to the principle of antitrust a certain grudging acceptance, for, as Hofstadter observed,

. . . visitations by the Department of Justice are a nuisance, lawsuits are expensive, and prosecution carries an unpleasant stigma, but the antitrust procedures can be considered an alternative to more obtrusive regulation, such as outright controls on prices. At any rate, big business has never found it necessary or expedient to launch a public campaign against antitrust enforcement; the pieties at stake are too deep to risk touching.[15]

Nevertheless, in the specific case business executives tend to attack the antitrust laws and the antitrust officials, apparently regarding the latter as enemies, as self-seeking or envious bureaucrats who operate without adequate controls from policymakers at the highest levels. They also regard the antitrust laws as vague, inconsistent, and generally opposed to the public interest, at least as the laws are administered.

On the other side, antitrust officials often feel that they are desperately and forlornly fighting the good fight against heavy odds, including public apathy and political resistance, or at best against ambiguity. They often feel that theirs is a hopeless cause. In fact, antitrust policy does face exceptional uncertainties and confusions in a time of precarious balance between a competitive society and an organizational society. When William H. Orrick resigned as Assistant Attorney General in charge of the Antitrust Division of the Justice Department under President Johnson in 1965, he said he felt caught between the President's "be-kind-to-businessmen philosophy and the demands of old-line antitrusters for prosecution-as-usual." Similarly, as we have seen, Richard W. McLaren's career as Assistant Attorney General for antitrust in the Nixon administration came to an abrupt end in the wake of the consent decree allowing the ITT–Hartford merger, although Attorney General John Mitchell insisted that his successor would "be called upon to continue the same vigorous antitrust enforcement."

[15] Richard Hofstadter, "What Happened to the Antitrust Movement?" in Earl F. Chest, ed., *The Business Establishment* (New York, 1964).

Not long afterward Mr. Mitchell himself left the Justice Department to head the Committee to Re-elect the President. Former Secretary of Commerce Maurice Stans joined in a massive fund-raising and disbursement effort on behalf of Richard Nixon, as did Herbert Kalmbach, the President's personal lawyer, and others closely associated with the White House and the Justice Department. Large business corporations were pressed for political contributions, which are illegal under the elections laws. The 1972 campaign was remarkable for the solicitation by a political party of huge financial contributions from special-interest groups in exchange for preferred favors, not only to business corporations but also to such groups as the milk producers. As the experienced political observer Robert Bendiner has said, "Big interests have in fact tried often to buy the favors of government and from time to time have succeeded—it would take a fatuous innocence to be unaware of that—but for a party in power to go from corporation to corporation inviting bribery with threats and promises requires a new dimension in cynicism."[16]

VIII

The complex task of reconciling the opposing tugs toward a competitive economy and a highly organized one has been with us for a long time. In the eighteen-eighties, when Senator Sherman was campaigning for his antitrust act, he declared that "society is now disturbed by forces never felt before." If Congress refused to act, he warned, there would soon be "a trust for every production and a master to fix the price for every necessity of life."

[16] *The New York Times,* July 17, 1973.

But Andrew Carnegie was at the same time declaring that mass production involved heavy fixed charges and that a chaotic market would wreck huge industries, cause capital to be wasted and depleted, and prevent national industrial development. The days of Adam Smith were dead and gone, said Carnegie, before the American free-enterprise business ideology had hardened. James B. Dill, the lawyer who brought Carnegie and J. P. Morgan together to form the United States Steel Corporation, told Lincoln Steffens: "Trusts are natural, inevitable growths out of our social and economic conditions. You cannot stop them by force, with laws. They will sweep down like glaciers upon your police, courts, and States and wash them into flowing rivers. I am clearing the way for them."[17]

Politics and business inevitably drew closer as corporations grew in size and scope. Not all liberals saw this as an undesirable trend. In 1912 Herbert Croly (who was soon to found *The New Republic*) depicted the career of the great Republican political boss Mark Hanna as an effort to fuse business and government interests for the sake of the public welfare. "Of course," said Croly, "as a politician he could not help representing business because business was a part of himself—because business was in his eyes not simply money-making, but the most necessary kind of social labor." Hanna, said Croly, saw no evil in what he was trying to do; rather, he sought to keep alive "in his own policy and behavior the traditional association between business and politics, between private and public interest, which was gradually being shattered by the actual and irresistible development of American business and political life." Hanna, in Croly's view, saw the essential harmony between the interests of business and those of the whole community, and he sought to develop it.

[17] Lincoln Steffens, *Autobiography* (New York, 1931), p. 196.

37

But how could this be done? How could one avoid the danger that the harmonizing of public (that is, state) interests and private-business interests would not be done at the expense of the "common people," the workers and farmers?

This, as Croly saw it, had been the central issue in American politics from the beginning, in the classic debates between Alexander Hamilton and Thomas Jefferson. In *The Promise of American Life* Croly had seen in Hamilton, the proponent of a strong central government founded on the combination of business and state interests, his hero and in Jefferson, the advocate of a weak central government and of equality for every man, his villain:

... Hamilton's political philosophy was much more clearly thought out than that of Jefferson. He has been accused by his opponents of being the enemy of liberty; whereas in point of fact, he wished, like the Englishman he was, to protect and encourage liberty, just as far as such encouragement was compatible with good order, because he realized that genuine liberty would inevitably issue in fruitful social and economic inequalities. But he also realized that genuine liberty was not merely a matter of a constitutional declaration of rights. It could be protected only by an energetic and clear-sighted central government, and it could be fertilized only by the efficient national organization of American activities. For national organization demands in relation to individuals a certain amount of selection, and a certain classification of these individuals according to their abilities and deserts. It is just this kind of effect of liberty which Jefferson and his followers have always disliked and discouraged. They have been loud in their praise of legally constituted rights; but they have shown an instinctive and implacable distrust of intellectual and moral independence, and have always sought to suppress it in favor of intellectual and moral confirmity.[18]

[18] Herbert Croly, *The Promise of American Life* (New York, 1963), p. 44.

Did the American business community take a wrong turn when it accepted the Jeffersonian creed, a creed that was transmogrified into the American free-enterprise business ideology, with its strong antigovernment bias, its commitment to laissez-faire, its emphasis upon "rugged individualism"? Were these not doctrines that have become more and more inappropriate, not only to the efficient operation of the economic system but to the liberty of the individual in an age of industrialism?

American business leaders are coming again to the logic of the prophetic Virginia statesman Benjamin Watkins Leigh, who more than a century ago warned that "power and property may be separated for a time by force or fraud—but divorced, never. For so soon as the pang of separation is felt . . . property will purchase power, or power will take over property. And either way, there must be an end to free government."

But the problem is growing more difficult all the time because of the increasing size of both government and business. "Size," says Carl A. Gerstacker, chairman of the Dow Chemical Company, "should no longer be a governing factor in government decisions concerning business." The problems of our times, he adds, will require "greater, bigger organizations than we now have . . . for their solution." In effect, he would resolve the difficult business-government issue simply by having government get out of the way. What is needed, says Mr. Gerstacker, is not merely international and multinational corporations but what he calls "anational" corporations, and he confesses that he has "long dreamed of buying an island owned by no nation," establishing his corporation's world headquarters "on the truly neutral ground of such an island, beholden to no nation or society."

Quite a few multinational corporate executives apparently

39

share Mr. Gerstacker's dream, although they describe it less openly and candidly. But after the collapse of the Penn Central Railroad, the bail-out of the Lockheed Aircraft Corporation, the merger of ITT and Hartford Fire, and ITT's political activities in Chile—in all of which cases the common issue was the influence of great corporations over governments—one might almost think that a solution to the most serious problems of modern industrial societies would point to an emergence of the "acorporate nation" rather than the "anational corporation."

It has become increasingly clear that specific actions will be required to bring corporate power under more effective control and to prevent it from distorting national priorities and subverting the public interest. President Eisenhower was speaking of only one major sector of the American political economy, the sector he christened "the military-industrial complex," when he said its "total influence—economic, political, even spiritual—is felt in every city, every statehouse, every office of the Federal Government." While recognizing the imperative need for this development, said Mr. Eisenhower, "we must not fail to comprehend its grave implications. Our toil, resources, and livelihood are all involved; so is the very structure of our society." His words gain still greater weight when the problem is seen to be, not just the military-industrial complex, but the overall corporate-government complex. The overriding issue is how to prevent powerful special interests from frustrating the democratic process.

The issue is difficult to solve because all the clear, simple extremes are unworkable. Given modern industrial technologies, this country cannot go back to the highly atomistic, competitive model of the early nineteenth century, even if it were willing to accept the workings of the marketplace as the arbiter of all social values and outcomes. But the experience of totalitarian and democratic societies alike demonstrates that the mere substitution of the power of big government (especially corrupt government) for that of big business and the marketplace is no solution, or is much worse than no solution.

The crucial task facing the United States and other democratic societies is not only to find workable answers between the extremes—to limit concentrations of corporate power without undermining the efficiency of business, and to permit the market to allocate resources insofar as possible—but also to use adequate resources to achieve socially desirable purposes, in response to the democratically exercised choices of the society.

There is no magic formula for reconciling those aims. Instead, this nation and all others must seek to diffuse power by a great many measures. The antitrust laws and their administration must indeed be strengthened and vigorously employed to reduce the dominance of economic giants and at the same time to make the economic system more efficient. The myth that maximum size means maximum efficiency has been debunked not only by a great deal of economic analysis but by such recent events as the Penn Central debacle. And if the ITT case does nothing else, it at least illustrates one of the major reasons for concern about corporate size: the political power to bend the law to their purposes that great financial assets convey upon corporation heads. The antitrust laws were intended not only to prevent the misuse of market power but also to keep a free society from suffering from certain moral, social, and political effects that might stem from highly concentrated economic strength. Powerful corporations can gain access to the highest officials in the Justice Department or the White House, as lesser persons or businesses cannot; they

41

can use their connections with politicians from all over the country, since they operate in virtually every state, to bring pressure on administrators, legislators, and regulators; they can impair both political freedom and economic diversity. The nation would be well served by a renewed effort on the parts of courts and Congress to break up undue concentrations of economic (and political) power and to expose the entire antitrust process, especially the negotiation of consent decrees, to the light of day.

Corporate behavior needs more effective surveillance and criticism. The traditional regulatory agencies have too often assimilated the policies, attitudes, and even interests of the industries they are supposed to regulate. This has resulted from the common shifting of high-level staff and commissioners between the regulatory agencies and the regulated companies,[19] as well as from the fact that the regulated industries provide so much of the data and expert analyses on which the regulatory commissions depend.

New regulatory institutions are required, whose aims would be to spur competition rather than to act as screens for monopolies (or even as agents for the monopolists or oligopolists). They should have as their mission the protection of consumers' interests, not producers' interests, taking their cue from the pioneering work of public-interest groups in the areas of law, economics, and the natural environment.

[19] For instance, in the case of the Federal Communications Commission, of 33 commissioners who served between 1945 and 1970, 21 joined companies in the communications industry after their FCC service, and most of the other 11 left the FCC to retire. Of 32 high-level staff officials, during the same period, 13 left the FCC to join communications companies. Four FCC commissioners came from communications companies, as did 13 high-level staff officials. Roger G. Noll, Merton J. Peck, and John J. McGowan, *Economic Aspects of Television Regulation* (Washington, 1973), p. 123.

IX

In the early nineteen-seventies many Americans seemed to have lost faith in the ability of government to improve their lives or anybody else's. There was a wave of antipathy toward many forms of public goods and services, including not only "welfare" and "urban redevelopment" but even parks and schools, the public goods par excellence.

The conflict over bussing was merely the most publicized aspect of a widespread dissatisfaction with public education. Schools became institutions non grata in many places. When a crowd turned out in near-zero weather to protest New York City's plan to build a new mid-Queens high school, a city spokesman commented that the nearby communities simply did not want high-school students traveling through their areas. School insurance costs soared; some schools found their policies cancelled. In Congress Representative Jonathan Bingham of New York introduced a safe-schools act, commenting: "The problem of crime in the schools has grown to such proportions that it now threatens the very viability of our educational system. You can't have good education when children are afraid to walk in the halls or go to the bathroom." Thefts began to plague many schools, even in affluent communities.

Parks were seen as public menaces. It is instructive to recount a debate that took place at a meeting of Community Planning Board No. 3 on Staten Island. At issue was the disposition of Reeds Basket Willow, a thirty-acre saucer-shaped parcel of virgin bramble on Todt Hill, which was wanted by the City Parks Department. Robert J. Rofrano, an officer of the Chapin Avenue

Civic Association, voiced the dominant community view: "We don't want any sort of park. We all have our own parks in the form of backyards. We feel that when property is given to a governmental agency it becomes public, which we don't want. . . . Even if the city promises to make it a nature preserve, what would keep them from using the land for public housing once they got it?"

Contempt for public services showed up in many ways. On the Long Island Railroad, a line serving commuters to New York City, fare-cheating in the form of ticket altering and counterfeiting became a major problem. The losses were estimated at $10 million per year, or $40,000 per commuting day. Jules Bernstein, president of the Central Island Commuters Association, had little sympathy for the railroad. "The commuter is a lost sheep," he said. "He is absolutely powerless. The Transit Authority is unresponsive and arrogant, and the unions are totally indifferent to the quality of the service they render. So the rider gets a little satisfaction from cheating the railroad out of a few bucks."

In the subways, not only in New York but in Philadelphia, Boston, and other cities, graffiti were epidemic. New technology —Magic Markers and spray-painting cans—enabled graffiti artists, mostly teenagers, to go beyond the advertising billboards accessible to ballpoint pens and assail cars, station ceilings, and trackside walls. Removing the smears was costing the City of New York a half a million dollars a year, every station porter spending an hour a day on it. The graffiti were attacked according to subject matter: "We go for the obscenity first, then anything racist," said a subway superintendent. "Then the innocuous identification stuff."

In Washington, D.C., the John F. Kennedy Center for the

Performing Arts became a showcase for public contempt for public goods—and for the American public's desire to convert them into private goods. Nan Robertson reported:

Crystal chandeliers have been stripped, swatches of rugs and curtains snipped away; faucets pried from bathroom basins. Costumes and parts of sets have been spirited away from backstage, and even the brass covers on electric outlets are disappearing.

All the ashtrays and salt and pepper shakers originally purchased for the center's three restaurants have been stolen, as well as "much china, glassware, silverware and linens," center spokesmen reported.

Tourists have walked out with plants, posters, paintings, directional signs and several thousand menus.[20]

In 1972 Connecticut was losing about $250,000 a year to motorists who were skittering through exact-change automatic turnpike tollbooths without paying. Instituting a system to catch the culprits, the state nabbed nearly 900 offenders in six weeks. "They would go by and stick their tongues out," said veteran toll collector Chester Nerkowski. "They just didn't care." On May 30, 1973, Connecticut gave up and decided to replace all toll machines with people, who were much better at catching cheaters.

X

If the public mood was antisocial or antisocialist, champions of capitalism could take only cold comfort, since it also seemed antigrowth—which made it, at least by implication, anticapitalist.

In Exeter, New Hampshire, for instance, citizens protested construction of the Rockingham National Bank on the site of Dudley

[20] *The New York Times,* Dec. 3, 1971.

House, a nineteenth-century structure of Federalist design. Allen B. Wright, president of the bank, contended: "We feel we are right. We have to do it. We're helping the town and we have already promised not to destroy the house but to move it. After all, this is the business district and it has to grow and we are offering to build a modern, new facility that will be an asset to the community." But members of the community felt otherwise. Robert H. Bates, an English teacher at Phillips Exeter Academy said, "What we are concerned about is not just Rockingham Bank, but the other bank and even the academy. We are protesting the way organizations which the citizens of this town cannot reach go around changing the whole character of the town." Such conflicts became widespread.

Politicians began to voice their worries about growth. In Atlanta, Georgia, Mayor Sam Massell ticked off the problems of his city: transportation and traffic, pollution of the Chattahoochee River, an obsolete airport, a rising crime rate, public housing, crowded schools, and disgruntled and underpaid policemen and firemen. "But we cannot stop growing populationwise," said the Mayor, "because then our municipal revenue becomes stabilized, and the present income is already insufficient to fund present services."

New Hampshire's Governor Walter Peterson—no anticapitalist —was also perturbed about the fruits of growth. "When all is said and done, the central problem of New Hampshire in the foreseeable future is growth," he said. "Growth produces enormous benefits and new opportunities, but it also contains the seeds of disaster. Growth puts houses where there were open spaces. It puts pollution into streams, it requires new schools for which the property taxes of the newcomers do not fully pay. It discourages rather than encourages the tourists who come for elbow room and clean air. It puts demands on state services above and beyond what the average citizen pays in."

Are ordinary people and politicians beginning to sense that a grave threat to humanity has now come in a most seductive and seemingly innocent form: mankind's sincere desire to be rich—and its command of technology to achieve that end?

Such is the thesis of the Club of Rome report, *The Limits to Growth,* whose authors, Dr. Dennis L. Meadows and a team from the Massachusetts Institute of Technology, used a computerized model to predict that, if present economic and population growth trends continue, there will be within a century an ecological disaster—and a precipitous fall in the world's population and its industrial capacity.

This tragedy is expected to result from the malignant feedbacks produced by an industrial system designed to provide humanity with ever-increasing benefits. More specifically, the Meadows model postulates that the creation of capital—real capital, in the form of factories, mines, generators, trucks, trains, planes—causes economic growth; that greater wealth and expanding technology cause population to mount, as death rates fall faster than birth rates; and that a greater population, producing and consuming more and more, pollutes the earth and exhausts its resources.

For a little while longer, the model indicates, the world system can go on agglomerating capital and people in urban sprawl, but finally a limit is reached. Why? Because population, capital, and pollution all grow at exponential rates; like money at compound interest, they double and double and double. But the earth itself, and its resources, do not.

But when will the limit be reached? No wholly scientific answer is yet possible. The real empirical job has not been done, and the complexity of modeling a reasonably reliable economic-social-physical-scientific-technological world system goes far beyond anything yet attempted.

In fact, questions must be raised about the imminence of the disaster the MIT team foresees and about the model and empirical data on which their predictions are based. They may have very greatly underestimated the rate at which the pool of resources for sustaining life can be expanded.

That was the basic error of their distinguished early nineteenth-century predecessor, the Rev. Thomas Malthus: the error of regarding resources as essentially a fixed pool rather than as a function of changing technology. Iron was not a resource at all before the Iron Age, nor coal before the Steam Age, nor uranium before the Nuclear Age; and the sun will burn a long time. Resources can grow exponentially, like population and income; in fact, since the Industrial Revolution usable resources have done so, step by step, with man's expanding knowledge.

Yet even an ever-expanding pool of resources can be poisoned. And, even if total disaster should not lurk around the corner, life in an ever-expanding industrial system can become wretchedly crowded, dirty, and mean. The danger may even be that man can accommodate himself to almost anything, however ugly. "The real horror, Kuprin," said Dostoevski, "is that there is no horror."

XI

The serious problems of late capitalism are not just corporate, governmental, technological, or environmental, but very personal. Great numbers of people are sick of anonymity and hunger for identity and community. But the ways in which a mass-production commercial system responds to such needs often seem cruelly ironic or pathetic.

For example, six million Americans now live in mobile homes, and the number is growing rapidly. In 1973 about 600,000 mobile homes were constructed—nearly one fourth of all homes built that year, and more than half of all homes costing under $25,000. Characteristically, the owner of a mobile home leases a space in a mobile-home park for a monthly rate, which varies greatly, depending on the services provided. Taxes are low, since in most states mobile homes are licensed and taxed as vehicles (with depreciation), not as real estate.

For this reason, however, communities have been loath to permit the establishment of such parks, since they would have to foot the bills for educating the residents' children. As a result, the trend has been toward large adult-only parks of about two-hundred or more spaces. Surrounded with five- or ten-foot walls, these self-contained communities are usually built around modern clubhouses and other common facilities, such as swimming pools and even golf courses. The spaces costing between $250 and $300 a month, they give their middle-income residents relatively cheap housing, with little upkeep or yard work. Children are forbidden, and the residents must be middle-aged.

More than 250,000 Californians live in some 5,100 mobile-home parks around the state. One of these is Lake Park, a community of 252 (in 1971) in Yorba Linda. Only 8 per cent of Lake Park's residents are retired, and the average age of a resident is about 52; most of the men commute to work like other suburban husbands. What distinguishes their lives from those of people living in conventional "stick" houses is the intense community life which begins once they are back within their ten-foot palisade.

All residents are automatically members of the Lake Park Club, and to keep them busy there is a perpetual whirl of parties, suppers, dancing, poker, and bingo. One resident, Len Armstrong, a burly office manager with a gray crewcut, commented, "Everything seems to be done in group fashion. There's no individuality. We have a lot of fun up in our group. We're known as the 'clean group,' and every night at quarter of nine I ring a cowbell, and that means to get into bathing suits. Then at nine o'clock I ring it again, and they all gather at our coach and go swimming."

Lake Park is governed by a series of rules that seem only less bizarre than the residents' ready acceptance of them. Cars cannot be parked on the streets, repaired in the park, or washed any place except in a shed provided for that purpose. Grandchildren are allowed to visit no more than two weeks a year. All homes and home equipment must be bought from the management. Above all, neighbors cannot be offended. Management reserves the right to ask couples to leave. "People want us to have that right," Ed Evans, one of Lake Park's three proprietors, said, "to be able to tell people they have to leave if they don't respect their neighbors, if they offend their neighbors."

Restrictions or no, Lake Park offers an escape from the oppressive impersonality or, perhaps, individualism of modern urban and suburban living. Harow E. Peck, president of the Lake Park Club, asserted: "If you're living in a conventional house, you're lucky to know people on either side of you. Here you know everybody. It just lends itself to the thing of wanting to know people—people want to know people."

The residents of Lake Park dissociate themselves entirely from the public life and concerns of Yorba Linda. One Lake Park resident explained, "This is a community within itself, but we love the surroundings. Still, as far as the community of Yorba Linda goes, you don't have much sense it's there."[21]

The city administrator of Yorba Linda agreed. "They've been occupied almost a year now," he said of the mobile homes of Lake Park, "and we don't even know they're there. No problem."

Lake Park is an exercise in nostalgia, a groping for a way back, or at least a way out. As such, it is far from unique in America these days.

A *New York Times* reporter, James T. Wooten, traveled to Savannah, Georgia, to investigate the pollution of the Savannah River; the Union Camp paper-bag plant was pouring thirty million gallons of waste per day into the river. Mr. Wooten reported the following conversation between two elderly residents of the city:

"It's a damned shame," said Homer Ray, a retired city employe who was born in Savannah 70 years ago. "I used to look out my window and watch porpoises jumping out of the river. . . . The pollution talk is just that . . . just talk. The politicians won't do anything that hurts them, and from what I understand, getting rid of pollution means more taxes and more taxes hurt politicians."

A companion on the bench interrupted. "You know what's polluting this city?" asked Jay Lee, an 82-year-old retired railroad conductor. "Nigras are polluting it, that's what," he said.

Mr. Ray did not seem to notice the new context. "I've come to the conclusion that pollution is like sin," Mr. Ray said. "Everybody's against it if you ask them where they stand, but everybody's got a little piece of it too."

Mr. Lee re-entered the conversation. "Once upon a time, they'd get off the sidewalks and let you pass," he said.

"Who?" askd Mr. Ray, slightly perturbed.

"The nigras, damn it, the nigras," replied Mr. Lee.

"Well, anyway," Mr. Ray continued, "maybe he has a point. He

[21] *The New York Times,* May 9, 1971.

51

can't do any more about the black people than anybody can do about the river. They ain't never going to be like he'd like for them to be, like they once were, and the river's never going to change now. Too much has already been done."

The two old men rose slowly from the bench and strolled away.

"That's all you see on television these days," Mr. Lee was muttering. "Nigras, that's all you see."[22]

Everyone is looking for his own escape. "Would you let your wife walk these streets at night?" asked a New York detective. Speaking in the squad room of a Manhattan precinct that had had a murder every third day, he was defending the right of city policemen to live with their families in the suburbs.

Some young people have sought a way out via the counter-culture. But what the Calley trial did to America's enthusiasm for the Vietnam war the Manson trial did to the counterculture's enthusiasm for the hippie lifestyle. By the time convictions were handed down for the Sharon Tate murders, the great American cultural awakening had been put through the wringer.

The Beatles broke up, and John Lennon summed up the disillusionment of a generation: "I no longer believe in myth, and Beatles is another myth. . . . I'm sick of all these aggressive hippies or whatever they are, the 'Now Generation,' being very up-tight with me. Either on the street or anywhere, or on the phone, demanding my attention, as if I owed them something. . . . They frighten me, a lot of up-tight maniacs going around, wearing peace symbols."

Even among young people nostalgia was in, and the new commercial craze was "golden oldies," vintage rock 'n' roll records from the early fifties into the sixties. Radio stations started switching to oldies' format and billing brand-new songs as

[22] *The New York Times,* January 28, 1971.

"future gold." In Boston, WCAS broadcast nothing but oldies and became the area's most popular station. WCAU in Philadelphia increased its audiences in two weeks from 58,000 to 250,000 by playing mostly older hits.

Dick Liberatore, whose "Big Beat Dance Party" is carried on Cleveland's WZAK, explained the phenomenon: "My audience wants to forget its problems and return to or at least recall those happy high-school times—the prom, no hair, no riots, no protests, the convertibles at the drive-in."

This was no serious search for the past but a sentimentalizing of it. But how to explain the huge dimensions of the nostalgia fad, which swept also into the revival of old films, old dances, the history of the Kennedy years or the Great Depression, a boom in the artifacts of the past, as "antiques"? Roger Rosenblatt suggests it is a consequence of affluence, a product of American progressivism:

Our affluence is, after all, an emblem of our faith in progress, in an onward-and-upward mobility whose principal, and national, caveat has been "Don't look back." When, however, we have gone as on or as up as we can or care to, we do look back, partly because we are secure enough to know that we won't actually fall back by doing so, and partly because we may be feeling more than a little guilty about the ruthlessness and thrust of our forward motion. Nostalgia, so used, becomes a form of absolution, an ideal form because the pain it causes is merely charming.

These varieties of regeneration and absolution account . . . for the nostalgia boom, particularly for the fact that the boom is ours. As the cultural aftermath to the war in Southeast Asia will persistently demonstrate, the two qualities of conscience we seek most avidly as a nation are instant innocence and painless guilt. These are the gifts nostalgia bears, but they are not what they appear, not the occasional daydream which lightens our present burdens, and not the handsome

53

hobbyhorse of our young imaginations. Instead, once again, are the armies of the nightmare.[23]

One thing one could be sure of: the nostalgia boom, like all others, would not last. In the capitalist culture, rapid obsolescence affects not only products but social trends (which are readily commercialized). It is all part of the process that Joseph Schumpeter called "creative destruction." Or, as Auden put it in *The Age of Anxiety,*

> . . . *The laws of science have*
> *Never explained why novelty always*
> *Arrives to enrich (though the wrong question*
> *Initiates nothing)* . . .[24]

XII

As some Americans, in the midst of accelerating economic and technological progress, were searching for surcease in the past, others were searching for God.

Among the far-out young the cultural movement for love and altered consciousness dissolved into a series of religious and semireligious cults. Many of these were Eastern in origin: the Meyer Baba movement, Sri Chinmoy, versions of the Japanese Soka Gakkai sect. Hare Krishna people, with their shaven heads and loose robes, their chanting and interminable shaking of bells, became a fixture on city streetcorners across the country. An estimated 175,000 Americans took up the transcendental meditation taught by the Maharishi Mahesh Yogi. But the largest of all the sects was the Jesus Movement.

The Jesus Movement had native American roots, but they did

[23] *The New York Times,* July 28, 1973.
[24] W. H. Auden, *The Age of Anxiety* (New York, 1946).

not lie in traditional fundamentalist Protestantism. Like the other cults, its origins were to be found in the Beat generation of the nineteen-fifties. *Beat* meant a musical beat, it also meant "beat up" or "exhausted," and most of all it meant "beatific." In 1958 Jack Kerouac told a television audience, "We love everything, Billy Graham, the Big Ten, rock and roll, Zen, apple pie, Eisenhower—we dig it all. We're in the vanguard of the new religion."

The hipsters had found in Jesus Christ the supreme symbol of the Beat man, caught between the cares of everyday life and spiritual transcendence. Allen Ginsberg wrote:

> . . . *I am a Seraph and I know not whither I go into the Void*
> *I am a man and I know not whither I go into Death— —*
> *Christ Christ poor hopeless*
> *lifted on the Cross between Dimension—*
> *to see the Ever-Unknowable!* . . .[25]

Lawrence Ferlinghetti put it more satirically:

> . . . *You're hot*
> *they tell him*
> *And they cool him*
> *They stretch him on the Tree to cool*
> *And everybody after that*
> *is always making models*
> *of this Tree*
> *with Him hung up*
> *And always crooning His name*
> *and calling Him to come down*
> *and sit in*
> *on their combo*
> *as if He is the king cat*
> *who's got to blow*

[25] Allen Ginsberg, *Kaddish and Other Poems Nineteen Fifty-Eight to Nineteen Sixty* (San Francisco, 1960).

> *or they can't quite make it*
> *Only he don't come down*
>
> *from His Tree . . .*[26]

In the nineteen-sixties hippies adopted the drugs and the transcendental pantheism of the Beats. Many used LSD, mescalin, and marijuana to "get into God." The invocation of a commune in Eugene, Oregon, began, "From the point of light within the mind of God let light stream forth into the minds of all brothers and sisters. Let light descend on earth."

As cracks in the counterculture began to appear, some spiritual seekers found the need for a less diffuse faith. Primitive Christianity exercised a strong appeal, and in the hills of California groups of young people began to imitate the lives of the apostles. In late 1971 an eight-page newspaper called *Great News* announced:

> People, this is it: Jesus took our load of ripoffs in His own flesh on the cross. Then he was buried, and three days later came back to life to show He wasn't a plastic God. There's more. He took off to heaven and someday soon He's coming back as Chairman of chairmen and Leader of leaders. One thing we can be sure of—He's gonna win big! Brothers and sisters, where are you at? You can cop out on the whole scene . . . You can bad-mouth Jesus . . . or you can let Him turn you on to heavy vibes of forever joy. Dig it![27]

Some fifty rock 'n' roll bands with names like "Resurrection," "The Galileans," and "The Armageddon Experience" appeared. They played a new kind of music termed "Gospel Rock," featuring such songs as "Going to Meet Jesus," "Born Again," and "Jesus, He's My Everything."

By early 1972 a three-year-old sect, the Children of God, had

---

[26] Lawrence Ferlinghetti, *A Coney Island of the Mind* (New York, 1958).

[27] Quoted in *The New York Times,* January 1, 1972.

founded eighty communes, growing faster than the Cistercian monasteries of the twelfth century. Enforcing strict sexual mores and bans on alcohol and drugs, the Children of God, known as COG, required all members to surrender their private possessions to the community in order to devote themselves "100 per cent to the Lord." No one was allowed to take a job in the outside world; within the communes, members memorized Scriptural passages as they performed assigned tasks, with separate "tribes" for such work as carpentry, mechanics, house cleaning, and cooking. Members adopted biblical names for themselves and carried their Bibles wherever they went, answering questions either by quoting a verse or looking one up.

In 1972 controversy surrounded the Children of God, as parents of some youthful converts accused the leaders of brainwashing their children and exploiting them. The parents found their children remote and uncommunicative when they came home to visit. Lynda Gilmour of Baltimore, an ex-COG, said, "They tell you your parents are your enemies, that the Devil is going to use them. They say hate, hate, hate the system—this abstract thing you can't see. They hate 'systemites'—anyone that's not with the Children of God."

Whether the leaders of COG sincerely intended an attack on "the system" or not, they had discovered in the nation's youth a desperate spiritual need. One called "Patience," the daughter of a senior vice-president of Mobil Oil, spoke for many when she described her spiritual conversion: "I had a very great spiritual hunger," she said. "I was looking for something more than what I found around me. My parents love me. They gave me everything I wanted and needed. But they didn't give me what I really needed, because they never told me about salvation, about Jesus." Yet, successful as it was, the Jesus Movement in 1972 was

about to be absorbed into a rising tide of traditional, fundamentalist evangelism.

During the nineteen-sixties American churches had been pulled
in the direction of social activism. Led by men like the Berrigan
brothers, James Groppi, William Sloane Coffin, and Martin
Luther King, religious organizations came to see themselves as
agents of reform and protest, supporting programs of civil rights
and opposing the Vietnam war. In the early nineteen-seventies
this was changing. "The social activists have been in the driver's
seat," said Albert van den Heuvel, a leader of the liberally
oriented World Council of Churches. "The next few years belong to those who are interested in recovering our spiritual and
Biblical roots."

In 1972, 130 religious groups signed up for Key '73, a movement
launched by a group of evangelist intellectuals, which aimed to
bring about a "Christian blitz." In June came Explo '72, a one-
week conference in Dallas, Texas, which was billed by Billy
Graham as a "Christian Woodstock."[28] Most of the 75,000 dele-
gated to Explo were white, neat, well-mannered, and sympathetic
to middle-class values; the long-haired Jesus "freaks" were far
outnumbered. In the mornings there were evangelical training
sessions; in the afternoons, discussion groups and Christian
"witnessing" on the streets of Dallas; and in the evenings dele-
gates congregated at the Cotton Bowl to hear performances by
singers Johnny Cash and Kris Kristofferson and speeches by Billy
Graham, the chief of Navy chaplains, a black evangelist, and
athletes, especially professional football players. The biggest ova-

[28] But there was still a yearning for the pristine Woodstock spirit. On
July 28, 1973, 600,000 rock-music fans gathered at the Grand Prix auto
racecourse at Watkins Glen, N.Y., in a one-day festival twice as large as
the 1969 Woodstock gathering. But "Woodstock this isn't," said a coed
from Montreal. "You can't recapture an ethereal spirit."

tion was reserved for Roger Staubach, quarterback of the Dallas Cowboys, who gave a short talk on "the game of life" in which "the goal line we must get across is our salvation" and "God has given us good field position."

Sharon Gallagher, a member of a Jesus group known as the Christian World Liberation Front in Berkeley, California, was among the minority that complained that the meeting had overlooked the social dimension of the Christian Gospel. "The whole thing reminds you of the Roman Coliseum," she said, standing behind the Cotton Bowl. "Except in those days the Christians weren't in the stands."

But, like the Emperor Constantine, the American "establishment" seemed to have appropriated Christianity. The astronaut James B. Irwin announced that he was resigning from the space program "to spend most of my time spreading the good news of Jesus Christ." In Saugus, California, youthful members of Christian sects were coming down from the hills to register Republicans, saying that the Democrats were too soft on drug use. "The conservative Republican viewpoint is the closest to the laws of God," said twenty-five-year-old Gail Bingham.

Spiro Agnew, before his fall from the vice presidency, called upon the traditional churches to welcome the "Jesus people"; he said they were seeking with youthful ebullience to make religion the central concern of American life.

Indeed, the money-changers in America's shopping centers were delighted to build their own temples and invite the ministers of God inside. South Hills Village, an enormous enclosed center in south suburban Pittsburgh, featured a counseling service, called Ministry in the Mall, run by a young Presbyterian clergyman. The huge Willowbrook Mall in Wayne, New Jersey, offered modern office space to Willowbrook Ministries, an ecumenical venture sponsored by national, regional, and local bodies of the Reformed Church in America, the United Presbyterian Church, the New Jersey Baptist Convention, the Lutheran Church, the United Church of Christ, the Episcopal Church, the United Methodist Church, and the Roman Catholic Church. The Rouse Corporation, who developed the Mall, were enthusiastic about the project because it fit the "total concept" of community that the corporation was trying to put across.

In Southern California and Florida ministers began preaching at drive-in churches, bringing the Word to acres of automobiles containing their casual parishioners, the message radioed in. "The genius of these churches is not just that the people may sit in their cars," declared a church father; "Drive-in churches offer a total program, many of them more full blown than the typical traditional church.":

It was all straight out of Nathanael West's *Miss Lonelyhearts:*

"What do you take us for—stinking intellectuals? We're not fake Europeans. We were discussing Christ, the Miss Lonelyhearts of Miss Lonelyhearts. America has her own religions. If you need a synthesis, here is the kind of material to use." [Shrike] took a clipping from his wallet and slapped it on the bar.

ADDING MACHINES USED IN
RITUAL OF WESTERN SECT . . .

Figures Will Be Used for Prayers for Condemned Slayer of Aged Recluse . . .
Denver, Colo., Feb. 2 (A.P.). Frank H. Rice, Supreme Pontiff on the Liberal Church of America, has announced he will carry out his plan for a "goat and adding machine" ritual for William Moya, condemned slayer, despite objection to his program by a Cardinal of the sect. Rice declared the goat would be used as part of a "sack cloth and ashes" service shortly before and after Moya's execution, set for the

week of June 20. Prayers for the condemned man's soul will be offered on an adding machine. Numbers, he explained, constitute the only universal language. Moya killed Joseph Zemp, an aged recluse, in an argument over a small amount of money.[29]

There is, it seems, a growing incompatibility between capitalism and religion—which is what infuses the attempts to bring religion to sports stadia, shopping malls, drive-in theaters, and the other temples of capitalism with such bathos.

That incompatibility was at first masked, as capitalism assimilated itself to (or was assimilated by) the Protestant churches during the Reformation. In his famous book *The Protestant Ethic and the Spirit of Capitalism* Max Weber contended that capitalism was the social counterpart of Calvinist theology; he put particular stress on the Calvinist concept of "a calling," which was not the state of life in which the individual had been placed by Heaven (Martin Luther's concept of "calling") but the earthly business he chose for himself, and which he had to pursue with religious fervor and responsibility. Thus the obligation to work hard, to be thrifty and sober, to save money and invest it prudently ("the Protestant ethic") acquired sanctity.

Yet there was a dialectical conflict between that calculating, abstemious, enterprising capitalist spirit and the religious faith on which it was nourished. For capitalism was intensely rational, and its cardinal instrument of rationality was money. As Schumpeter said, "capitalist practice turns the unit of money into a tool of rational cost-profit calculations, of which the towering monument is double-entry bookkeeping."

. . . Primarily a product of the evolution of economic rationality, the cost-profit calculus in turn reacts upon that rationality; by crystal-

[29] Nathanael West, *Miss Lonelyhearts* (New York, 1933; republished 1957), p. 73.

61

lizing and defining numerically, it powerfully propels the logic of enterprise. And thus defined and quantified for the economic sector, this type of logic or attitude or method then starts upon its conqueror's career subjugating—rationalizing—man's tools and philosophies, his medical practice, his picture of the cosmos, his outlook on life, everything in fact including his concepts of beauty and justice and his spiritual ambitions.[30]

It was not only the cost-profit rationality of capitalism that would ultimately subjugate the religious faith with which it allied itself but the very success of capitalist enterprise, and the vast affluence it would bestow upon its elect, that would make a mockery of the Protestant principles of asceticism, conservation, sobriety.

Max Weber foresaw that, although capitalism may have begun as "the practical idealism of the aspiring *bourgeoisie*,"[31] it would end as an orgy of materialism—particularly in the United States as the destined *reductio ad absurdum* of capitalism:

Since asceticism undertook to remodel the world and to work out its ideals in the world, material goods have gained an increasing and finally an inexorable power over the lives of men as at no previous period in history. Today the spirit of religious asceticism—whether finally, who knows?—has escaped from the cage. But victorious capitalism, since it rests on mechanical foundations, needs its support no longer. The rosy blush of its laughing heir, the Enlightenment, seems also to be irretrievably fading, and the idea of duty in one's calling prowls about in our lives like the ghost of dead religious beliefs. Where the fulfilment of the calling cannot directly be related to the highest spiritual and cultural values, or when, on the other hand, it need not be felt simply as economic compulsion, the individual generally abandons the attempt to justify it at all. In the field of its

[30] J. A. Schumpeter, *Capitalism, Socialism, and Democracy* (New York, 1942), pp. 123–124.

[31] Max Weber, *The Protestant Ethic and the Spirit of Capitalism* (New York, 1958), Foreword by R. H. Tawney, p. 3.

highest development, in the United States, the pursuit of wealth, stripped of its religious and ethical meaning, tends to become associated with purely mundane passions, which often actually give it the character of sport.

No one knows who will live in this cage in the future, or whether at the end of this tremendous development entirely new prophets will arise, or whether there will be a great rebirth of old ideas and ideals, or, if neither, mechanized petrification, embellished with a sort of convulsive self-importance. For of the last stage of this cultural development, it might well be truly said: "Specialists without spirit, sensualists without heart; this nullity imagines that it has attained a level of civilization never before achieved."[32]

Weber's bitter essay was first published in 1904. What reply shall Americans make today? Maybe Shrike's "What do you take us for—stinking intellectuals? We're not fake Europeans . . . America has her own religions"? or, in this age of European and Japanese affluence, anomie, high productivity and technology, mass consumption, and pollution, "You too"?

Such retorts are stupid. We must begin to provide more intelligent and humane answers.

[32] Max Weber, ibid., pp. 181–182.

PART TWO

Perspectives on Capitalism

STUDS TERKEL

Here Am I, a Worker

Discontent with what Max Weber called "the Protestant Ethnic" and what President Nixon calls "the work ethic" seems to be growing more intense in the United States and other industrial countries—even in the Soviet Union. The Communist Revolution was supposed to end alienation of workers by abolishing private ownership of the means of production, thereby ending capitalist exploitation of labor. But work alienation is reportedly as severe in the government-owned plants of the Soviet Union as it is in the West. Indeed, some of the most autocratic and repressive organizations in the West are state-owned.

All this repression has started to produce its explosions. The worst was probably the "events of May" in France in 1968, when students and workers virtually brought the economy and the state to a standstill. In the United States there has been an occasional explosion, such as the strike of enraged young workers at the hypermodern Lordstown, Ohio, plant of General Motors in early 1972. But American alienation has primarily taken the form of sullen "blue-collar blues," which have their white-collar analogue, as Studs Terkel, author of Hard Times *and other books, and interviewer on Chicago's WFMT, shows in this insightful piece.*

In our society (it's the only one I've experienced, so I cannot speak for any other) the razor of necessity cuts close. You must make a buck to survive the day. You must work to make a buck. The job is often a chore, rarely a delight. No matter how demeaning the task, no matter how it dulls the senses or breaks the spirit, one *must* work or else. Lately there has been a questioning of this "work ethic," especially by the young. Strangely enough, it has touched off profound grievances in others, hitherto silent and anonymous.

Unexpected precincts are being heard from in a show of discontent by blue collar and white. Communiqués are alarming concerning absenteeism in auto plants. On the evening bus the tense, pinched faces of young file clerks and elderly secretaries tell us more than we care to know. On the expressways middle-management men pose without grace behind their wheels, as they flee city and job.

In all, there is more than a slight ache. And there dangles the impertinent question: Ought there not to be another increment, earned though not yet received, to one's daily work—an acknowledgment of a man's *being*?

Steve Hamilton is a professional baseball player. At 37 he has come to the end of his career as a major-league pitcher. "I've never been a big star. I've done about as good as I can with the equipment I have. I played with Mickey Mantle and with Willie Mays. People always recognize them. But for someone to recognize me, it really made me feel good. I think everybody gets a kick out of feeling special."

Mike Fitzgerald was born the same year as Hamilton. He is a laborer in a steel mill. "I feel like the guys who built the pyramids. Somebody built 'em. Somebody built the Empire State

Building, too. There's hard work behind it. I would like to see a building, say The Empire State, with a foot-wide strip from top to bottom and the name of every bricklayer on it, the name of every electrician. So when a guy walked by, he could take his son and say, 'See, that's me over there on the 45th floor. I put that steel beam in.' Picasso can point to a painting. I think I've done harder work than Picasso, and what can I point to? Everybody should have something to point to."

Sharon Atkins is 24 years old. She's been to college and acridly observes: "The first myth that blew up in my face is that a college education will get you a worthwhile job." For the last two years she's been a receptionist at an advertising agency. "I didn't look at myself as 'just a dumb broad' at the front desk, who took phone calls and messages. I thought I was something else. The office taught me differently."

Among her contemporaries there is no such rejection; job and status have no meaning. Blue collar or white, teacher or cabbie, her friends judge her and themselves by their beingness. Nora Watson, a young journalist, recounts a party game, Who Are You? Older people respond with their job titles: "I'm a copy writer," "I'm an accountant." The young say, "I'm me, my name is so-and-so."

Harry Stallings, 27, is a spot welder on the assembly line at an auto plant. "They'll give better care to that machine than they will to you. If it breaks down, there's somebody out there to fix it right away. If I break down, I'm just pushed over to the other side till another man takes my place. The only thing the company has in mind is to keep that line running. A man would be more eager to do a better job if he were given proper respect and the time to do it."

You would think that Ralph Grayson, a 25-year-old black, has it made. He supervises twenty people in the audit department of a large bank. Yet he is singularly discontented. "You're like a foreman on an assembly line. Or like a technician sitting in a computer room watching the machinery. It's good for a person who enjoys that kind of job, who can dominate somebody else's life. I'm not too wrapped up in seeing a woman, 50 years old—white, incidentally—get thrown off her job because she can't cut it like the younger ones.

"I told management she was a kind and gentle person. They said, 'We're not interested in your personal feelings. Document it up.' They look over my appraisal and say: 'We'll give her about five months to shape up or ship out.' "

The hunger persists, obstinately, for pride in a man's work. Conditions may be horrendous, tensions high, and humiliations frequent, yet Paul Dietch finds his small triumphs. He drives his own truck, interstate, as a steel hauler. "Every load is a challenge. I have problems in the morning with heartburn. I can't eat. Once I off-load, the pressure is gone. Then I can eat anything. I accomplished something."

Yolanda Leif graphically describes the trials of a waitress in a quality restaurant. They are compounded by her refusal to be demeaned. Yet pride in her skills helps her through the night. "When I put the plate down, you don't hear a sound. When I pick up a glass, I want it to be just right. When someone says, 'How come you're just a waitress?' I say, 'Don't you think you deserve being served by me?' "

Peggy Terry has her own sense of pride and beauty. Her jobs have varied with geography, climate, and the ever-felt pinch of circumstance. "What I hated worst was being a waitress, the way you're treated. One guy said, 'You don't have to smile, I'm gonna give you a tip anyway.' I said, 'Keep it, I wasn't smiling

70

for a tip.' Tipping should be done away with. It's like throwing a dog a bone. It makes you feel small."

Ballplayer. Laborer. Receptionist. Assembly-line worker. Truck driver. Bank official. Waitress. What with the computer and all manner of automation, add scores of hundreds of new occupations and, thus, new heroes and antiheroes to Walt Whitman's old anthem. The sound, though, is no longer melodious. The desperation is unquiet.

Perhaps Nora Watson has put her finger on it. She reflects on her father's work. He was a fundamentalist preacher, with whom she had been profoundly at odds.

"Whatever, he was, he was. It was his calling, his vocation. He saw himself as a core resource of the community. He liked his work, even though his family barely survived, because that was what he was supposed to be doing. His work was his life. He himself was not separate and apart from his calling. I think this is what all of us are looking for, a calling, not just a job. Most of us, like the assembly-line worker, have jobs that are too small for our spirit. Jobs are not big enough for people."

Does it take another, less competitive, less buck-oriented society to make one match the other?

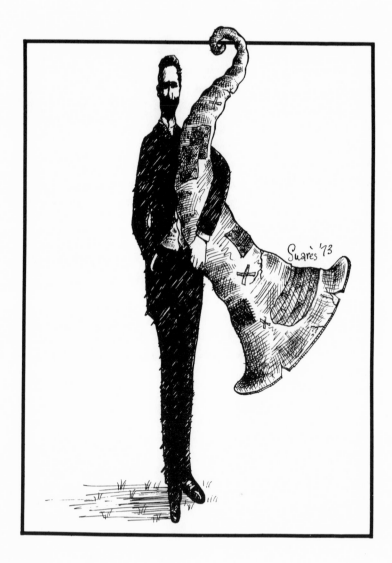

GILBERT SORRENTINO
Empty, Empty Promises, Promises

*Does the artist ever love his patron? Reading Shakespeare's rather
cloying dedications to his noble lords, one may suspect the contrary.
Did he resent his aristocratic masters more or less than Joyce Carey's
Gulley Jimson resented the capitalist art dealers? It was certainly less
than Solzhenitsyn resents the Politburo.*

*The artist characteristically says he wants only two things from
his patron, money and freedom, although it is obvious he would like
a third: appreciation. Capitalism does pretty well by the arts on the
first two counts, less well on the third. The artist is often regarded
as a bit of a freak or a kook, and some important work is doubtless
ignored or underprized. The market is highly erratic in how it be-
stows its favors upon artists and writers; some may grow rich beyond
their deserts—it was Jean Cocteau who said that fashion is what is
beautiful today and ugly tomorrow, and art is what is ugly today
and beautiful tomorrow—while other truly great artists, as Gilbert
Sorrentino says, using James Joyce as his example, may dwell in
poverty.*

*How to distribute the largesse of the system more fairly among
creative talents is an unsolved problem of capitalism, since no one,
especially the artists themselves, wants to give up freedom for either
state or corporate control.*

Sorrentino's latest novel is Imaginative Qualities of Actual Things.

73

This picture of the young James Joyce in 1906, working as a clerk in a Roman bank, might as well serve as a rubric for this piece, which will deal with capitalism: "Does capitalism do anything beautiful for us? Can it create anything of lasting value in the arts? Can it do beautiful things?" Joyce, in his ragged patched pants, sweating in Rome, surrounded by money—what is that but the true Joycean touch, right out of *Finnegans Wake*? It could be, in fact, another stroke in his portrait of Shem the Penman. It has the elements of darkly comic Irish humor: the ne'er-do-well artist with brain afire. In a minute he'll get drunk, sing a dirty song, and fall on his face.

The reader will see that my conception of capitalism has to do only with its effect on the single, the unique, human being. Or let me put it this way: I'll give you the Seagram Building if you'll bring back Baudelaire and give him a hundred dollars a week. Capitalism in its relationship to the arts is like love: it has no meaning worth our attention once it moves out of that area in which real people with real faces, bodies, and names live. Abstract ideas are at the root of wars, famine, and destruction. Think of the sins of nationalism. Did you ever eat a nationalism? Capitalism is the same smeary sort of thing. It cannot really *do* anything for Tom, Dick, or Harry. It is a kind of idea into which power can crawl. One can then expect it to do things, one can insist that it produces a William Calley, as one can insist Marxism produced Stalin. If you believe this, you believe in "historical inevitability." I can't hear you as you ride away on your hobby-horse.

A configuration to ponder: the Metropolitan Museum and the Marlborough Galleries. What is going on here? Millions being traded back and forth, men who probably have a great deal of trouble sewing on a button or sweeping a floor raking in sawbucks by the pound. It's all business. And right over here, ladies and gents, some numbskull of a painter ("Who *asked* him to be a painter?" a voice grumbles) who can't make the rent for a studio big enough for him to paint and house his family in. Tell it to the Marines, do I hear you say? Okay. If this equation doesn't say capitalism plus art equals many rich dealers and one broke painter, what does it say?

Don't get me wrong. I don't think that government, whatever that is, should "subsidize" the artist. Government tends to think in terms of things being useful, and with art, they are lost in the stars. We'll put that dam right over here, Charlie, right? Then the valley will be green, the floods, etc., everything wonderful, right! Now, this poem—what about this damn thing? Get it out to the People! Right! A little culture, a little beauty! Brighten the corner where you are! By God, it's as good as a regular-guy priest and Bob Hope rolled into one if we play our cards right! The idea is that art is a hammer or saw that is used to build culture and hope and high thoughts in the minds and hearts of the unwashed. Well, I say to hell with it. Art is no missionary casting about for souls to save, nor an entertainer traveling far and wide to laugh it up. If you want it, you have to go and get it—it's distressingly still. It's also useless. You say your marriage is breaking up, you have a bleeding ulcer, your son is a heroin addict? Here's a Van Gogh—take a good look at it. Right! Now, read these poems by this guy, what's-his-name. Rimbaud. Now, how do you feel? Your marriage is worse than ever? Your stomach is burning through your belt buckle? Your son ran away from Synanon? Van Gogh and poor Arthur didn't do anything for you, is that it? It's no surprise—one always suspected that artists couldn't pull their weight.

Art has no use. Art is beautiful. Art is beholden to no man. Art is also made by artists. Ah, there's the rub. These latter eat, sleep, need warmth in winter, clothes, etc. Patches on their pants, all the rest. Whatever the noble plumber needs, so does the noble poet, "Capitalism" doesn't do anything for this obscure human being except allow him to work at a job that will pay the rent and buy his chuck steak. It does for the artist what it does for any man. As far as its doing "beautiful things," it may do them by default, or accidentally. If the Chase Manhattan wants some art on its officers' walls, then the painter who made this art gets some money. (There is a chance he might even be a good painter.) The Chase Manhattan gets some money to the artist. This is known as Capitalism in Action. But who can care about the fact of the pictures on the bank's walls? The Chase Manhattan should have pictures of currency on its walls, or far-seeing past directors, eyes fixed on the Eternal Truths, or even group photos like those great images of corn one sees in saloons in places like Brooklyn—you know the kind I mean (or do you? Hello! Are there any people out there who were born and raised in New York? Hello? Hello?): GALLAGHER'S 12TH ANNUAL CLAMBAKE, RYE BEACH. In the pictures are longshoremen, cops, firemen, truck drivers, mailmen and assorted clerkish losers from the "financial district" smiling drunkenly through the boilermaker haze and sunlight, their wives gallantly supporting them. Well, there's no art there, brother, nor should there be, just as there should be none on the walls of Chase Manhattan's offices. I mean to say that a Clyfford Still would be just as ridiculous on Chase Manhattan's wall as on Gallagher's. If you don't believe me, ask Still.

I see myself in those offices, pictures worth a half-million dollars glittering beneath their ten thousand dollars' worth of special lighting. I have a hole in my hat, no job, sixty bucks in the bank, and my only collateral, as my dear mother used to say, is my right arm with the blood dripping. I'm looking for a loan to pay the rent. Then I say "I'm a writer," the magic words that propel me into the street, courteously, of course. Once there, I can look at the Seagram Building, brought to you by Capitalism, Inc. Somehow, capitalism has failed me, and I produce this same art the Chase Manhattan reveres in one of its many forms. But their taste! Their sensibility! Their love and care! Can it be that capitalism and art go hand in hand only if one of the hands is not made of flesh and blood?

In any event, I'm an artist, for better or worse. I've had many jobs, hard and easy, reasonably boring and crushingly so. In this way I have survived through capitalism's largesse, i.e., paychecks. That is the something beautiful that capitalism has done for me. If I were a painting, I'd be worth more, but let that go. As for the Seagram Building, I can take it or leave it. People work there, moving papers around. They watch the clock, flirt, cringe, complain. Ho-hum. It's got nothing to do with me. I have nothing against this building, but have here used it analogously in homage to Joyce's famous cow, made by a man hacking in fury at a block of wood. Stephen Dedalus asked if it was a work of art. He didn't answer his question, but I know the answer. Or, to end on a, for me, uncharacteristically Zen note: *Question:* Is the Seagram Building an example of capitalism doing something beautiful for us? *Answer:* Buy James Joyce a pair of pants.

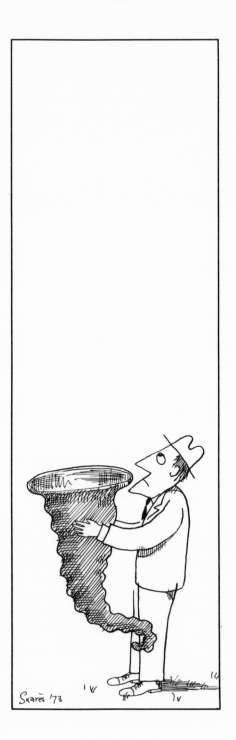

THOMAS CARVEL
Land of Opportunity? Damned Right!

Lovers of the market economy insist that it is much fairer than any alternative system, since it rewards the determined and capable person for what he can do, what he can contribute, rather than for who he is or who his parents were or even how much wealth or other gifts they passed on to him.

This is how the American economic system still looks to Thomas Carvel, founder and chairman of the board of the ice-cream-manufacturing Carvel Corporation, who won the Horatio Alger Award in 1957.

Today I met a man who asked, "Do you really believe that the opportunities in this country are the same as they were in your youth?"

I was reminded of the day that I was addressing a class at a local college, and one of the students said, "Mr. Carvel, I don't believe that the opportunities in this country today can be compared to what they were even fifty years ago. After all, you went to Hartsdale on Central Avenue and started with a little bit of a broken-down trailer and built a business from that."

I thought for a while, and then I asked several other students their opinions on this matter. They all seemed to concur with their classmate. What they said basically was that the opportunity in this country has been exhausted. When our country was founded, there was more opportunity than there is now, because the further back we go, the fewer were the developments, the fewer were the techniques, and the less was absolute knowledge.

And, in answer to the question, I said to the young man, "Did you consider that when I was your age we didn't have jet airplanes?" We didn't know too much about our own universe. The moon itself was a mystique, thought to be made of cheese. We didn't know a surface existed on the moon, or that we were capable of negotiating a trip there with living human beings. The various technologies and developments and expansions of the entire universe are so far greater today that the challenges are unbelievable.

Opportunities, in this country? The world's greatest. However, do we intend to preserve those opportunities and use them to our advantage?

Or, are we going to permit them to be destroyed by someone who thinks he has a better format, that every other country is better than ours, and every other political system is better, and we should change this and copy that?

The privilege of doing your own thing and creating something for yourself to include a business is the most wonderful part of this country. We are permitted to do it. Were we not permitted this luxury, people like myself and millions of others in this country, who have been free to develop businesses if they so chose, would be denied the opportunity of expanding their own thoughts or opportunity. We were at the right place at the right time and prospered with a business.

In answer to a question, "Are there still opportunities in this country?" there are millions of opportunities now that did not exist years ago. The opportunity need not be questioned. The facts are that in 200 years we surpassed the Greek and Roman Empires, and all the major countries in the world. How was that done?

It was done exactly the way we have expanded in the franchise industry. Our Carvel business consists of hundreds of families who have saved their monies all their lives to enjoy the fruits of a business. We provide them with a customer acceptance, a method and technique, and teach them how to do it. They, then, are Carvel. They, then, are individuals running a business of their own. Basically, this was the principle of the United States. It permitted you freedom of operating a business. It permitted you the right to purchase the property and build a business or build a house. There are many countries where even these simple freedoms do not exist.

Is there opportunity in this country? I would certainly say yes. When you think that, not many years ago, because my father did not speak English well, he talked to me in Greek, yet he spoke two other languages, and that when he spoke to me in Greek, the kids called me a greaseball—and when I think that a greaseball was privileged to do his own thing and to work as he saw fit, where he saw fit, and how he saw fit—the credit must go to America. We were privileged by the freedoms and the opportunities of this unbelievable country. I asked myself this question: Would I have been better off were I brought up in Greece, which was my father's native country? And my conclusion is: No way.

Now then, were I not able to succeed in my business here,

would it be right for me to blame this country for my inadequacies or failures? I know people of all races and religions and colors who are basically successful within their own right.

Let's think about today and tomorrow, and our future in this country. That which we take for granted would be the greatest gift bestowed upon the peoples of many other nations. What is the strength of America? Basically it's people. In reality, was not the overwhelming majority of those people responsible for our country's growth, descendants of ancestors of foreign birth? Yet we have risen to become the strongest, richest, most powerful nation on the face of the earth. By working together, growing together, and benefiting together, we can insure the berth America now occupies will remain implacable. If anyone asks me if America is still the land of opportunity, my response is "You're damned right it is."

EDWIN KUH
Who Gets What and Why

Edwin Kuh, professor of economics at the Massachusetts Institute of Technology, who was an economic adviser to Senator George Mc-Govern during the 1972 presidential campaign, contends that a genuine political democracy and real equality of opportunity are impossible of attainment in the face of extreme differences in wealth.

In the wake of Senator McGovern's defeat Mr. Kuh recognizes that the nation is in no mood to tackle the job of redistributing income on any large scale; on the contrary, he suggests, it clings to the ideology of individualism and identifies the interests of ordinary individuals with those of the great corporations. But he argues that equal opportunity cannot be achieved in the United States—especially for those trapped by racism and other forms of social and economic discrimination—until large concentrations of wealth are broken up and the tax laws reformed so as to redistribute income and wealth.

What is the present distribution of income and wealth in the U.S.A.? Wealth is distributed much more unevenly than income; thus, the richest 10 per cent of the population receive 29 per cent of personal income but own 56 per cent of the national wealth, while the poorest 10 per cent receive 1 per cent of the income and are in debt, to boot. At the top of the wealth distribution 1 per

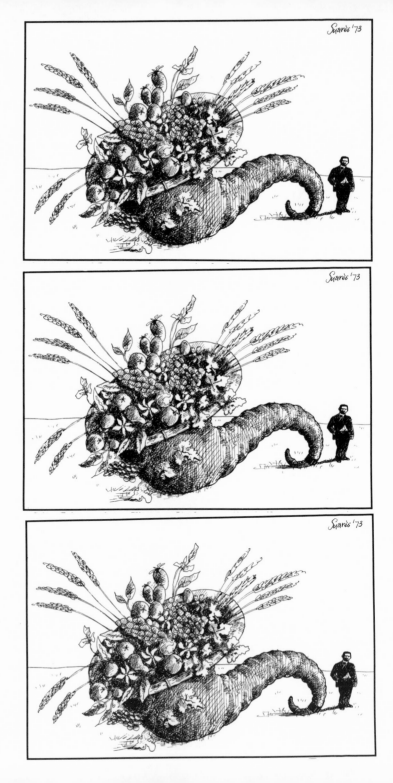

cent of the wealth-holders own 25 per cent of physical and financial wealth. Among those with incomes in excess of $100,000, inherited wealth amounts to 57 per cent of total assets.

Despite the extreme inequality that now prevails, two principles embedded in the American tax structure are that taxes should be levied according to ability to pay and that at least some income should be redistributed to the poor. Taxes paid by the prosperous are used, in a variety of ways, to help the poor. But apart from the need to help the poor, there are other cogent reasons to tax the rich at higher rates and to work for genuine tax reform. First, massive concentrations of wealth or income make a mockery of political democracy. Second, real equality of opportunity is impossible in the presence of extreme wealth or extreme poverty. Reducing inequality at the top would thus yield benefits to the middle class as well.

"One person, one vote" is a sham—for the middle class and poor alike—when the rich can buy political influence. When the President of the United States told an assembly of wealthy Texans that the petroleum percentage depletion allowance should, if anything, be increased, the outpouring of warmth and financial support was predictably generous. The Federal Election Campaign Act of 1972 was a small step in the right direction, but any law intended to curb the undue political influence of the affluent will be readily evaded as long as large concentrations of wealth exist. It would, moreover, be naïve to focus attention on rich individuals to the exclusion of giant corporations. While a saving grace of the present system is that business interests often conflict, it is also true that they coalesce on such basic issues as stiffer capital-gains taxes, inheritance taxes, and tax reform in general.

The second reason for supporting stiffer inheritance and income taxes has to do with equality of opportunity. Equal opportunity is more of a reality in America than in most countries. Yet it is, and will remain, in part a mirage until large concentrations of wealth are broken up. Large inheritances are the antithesis of equal opportunity. The more unequal the distribution of income and wealth, the more closely we approach Anatole France's characterization of equality before the law—the prohibition of rich and poor alike from sleeping under bridges. While the notion of equality of opportunity does not imply that income and wealth should be equally distributed, extreme concentrations represent an insurmountable barrier to those below and a permanent crutch for those above.

Rational arguments for income and wealth inequality boil down to the need "to preserve incentives." This proposition is usually warped into arguments for the status quo: that American capitalism will come to an end should these privileges be curtailed, or that economic growth will grind to a halt if incentives are tampered with. In the United States, however, the growth of economic productivity has been substantially greater since World War II than it was before, yet the tax burden has been much greater. Abroad, economic growth rates vary greatly, from 10.8 per cent in Japan to 1.8 per cent in Great Britain (annual compound growth rates in real gross national product for the most recent available five-year period), yet income distributions are strikingly similar among the advanced industrial countries. Clearly, the processes of growth are much more complex than the incentive argument would suggest. While care is required not to kill the goose that lays the golden egg, the incentive argument in current discussions about income distribution merely cloaks self-interest in the guise of general welfare.

There is widespread agreement in principle in the United

States on the need to redistribute some income from the rich to the poor, since the less fortunate should be provided for as a matter of right in a just society. The advocates of redistribution cover the political spectrum from conservatives such as Milton Friedman and Republicans such as President Nixon (early in his first term) to Democratic liberals such as Senators Kennedy, McGovern, and Ribicoff. The recommended programs are as varied as the proponents: negative income taxes for those with children or for everyone; or more emphasis on jobs rather than on income maintenance; or support in certain categories through subsidized housing, compensatory education, or health insurance.

The attainment of meaningful redistribution of income and wealth through sensible tax reform seems remote at this time, because agreement in principle conflicts with willingness to pay. Congressional rejection of President Nixon's Family Assistance Plan proposal, together with its abandonment by the President, reflect the country's mood accurately enough. Part of the reason, as I have argued, is the ability of the wealthy to buy into the political process, but there is more. One component of American ideology is a belief in rugged individualism. However admirable in its own right, this article of faith has been distorted by the apologists of privilege, who falsely identify the interests of ordinary individuals with those of the wealthy and virtually immortal corporations as well.

Another factor, racism, is also powerfully at work. While a majority of the poor are white, blacks are often seen as the main beneficiaries of income redistribution. Hence an alliance between wealthy and middle-income whites (many of whom are not racist) has grown stronger. In the process popular attention has shifted to divisive social issues at the lower end of the income distribution and away from the pernicious effects of extreme disparities at the upper end of the distribution. Yet until the incomes of the wealthy and the middle classes are made more nearly equal, true democracy and equal economic opportunity will suffer.

ANDREW GLYN
The Wage-Push Crisis of Capitalism

Andrew Glyn, a fellow and tutor at Corpus Christi College, Oxford, has stirred up much controversy with his thesis that British capitalism faces a new crisis as a result of the mounting wage pressures of increasingly militant trade unions. Since employers, bound by the constraints of foreign competition in home markets and abroad, cannot pass on higher wages by raising prices as much, their profits decline, investment stagnates, and capitalism itself is threatened with collapse, according to the argument developed by Glyn and his coauthor Bob Sutcliffe in Capitalism in Crisis. *They say organized labor must either accept a curtailment of its power to push up wages (as through government controls) or fight to overthrow the capitalist system. As members of the New Left, they urge the latter course.*

In the following piece Glyn suggests that capitalism in the United States also faces a wage-push crisis. His American ally, Professor Edward J. Nell of the New School for Social Research, contends that the tendency of profits to be forced downward in this country whenever full employment is approached must inevitably provoke a political defense of profits, and that, in turn, must involve an attack on labor. "Such an attack cannot simply be an attack on wages; profits will not be safe unless the power of labor to push up money wages is curtailed. So the attack must be made on the rights and privileges of collective bargaining. We have seen this begin under the Nixon administration . . . The lessons for the United States labor movement

Suarès '73

are plain." Neither British nor American labor, however, shows any sign of being converted to a revolutionary philosophy by these trends, which have a factual basis; instead there is widespread grumbling about, but acceptance of, continuing inflation.

The British economy is in a period of acute crisis. After two decades of a diminished share in world trade, the last few years saw inflation accelerating to around 10 per cent per annum, combined with feebler growth and unemployment rising above the million mark. Much less well known is the acute profitability crisis, which leaves British capitalism—that is, the system of production for private profit—literally struggling for survival.

After a slow decline since the war, between 1964 and 1970 the proportion of the value of corporate output going to profits (after depreciation but before tax) slumped from 21.2 per cent to 12.1 per cent, while the post-tax rate of profit fell by a similar proportion. The profits squeeze was caused by the interaction of two forces that have grown out of the postwar development of capitalism.

First, there has been the pressure by the British working class for higher wages, stoked by the expectations created by the modest, but steady, gains in real wages in the fifties and early sixties and by the growing realization by the working class of its own industrial strength. But money wage increases would not threaten profitability without some constraint which prevents firms from passing on the higher costs in the form of higher prices. This constraint has been the competition faced by British capital from overseas.

In fact, British capital has by no means been the only sufferer from this process whereby profitability is squeezed between wage increases and international competition. Indeed Italy, after the

91

"miracle" of the fifties and early sixties, has suffered the most serious profits squeeze of all since the "hot autumn" of 1969. Nor has the United States escaped entirely, for the profit share fell from 22.9 per cent in 1964 to 17.5 per cent in 1970, more than can be explained by cyclical factors. It remains to be seen whether the devaluation of the dollar, together with the wage and price policy, will reverse this decline.

Capitalists have tried to restore profit margins in Great Britain by faster inflation, by a merger boom, by a massive wave of redundancies (layoffs) aimed at reducing costs, and with the effect that productivity leaped up. Business investment, which initially was propped up by a massive increase in borrowing, has recently declined substantially. But British capital has been quite incapable of restoring the situation without using state power. The taxation of workers has been increased and the resources redistributed to capital through lower corporation tax. Prices charged by nationalized industries have been held down to provide cheap inputs for the private sector. Unemployment was increased in a completely unsuccessful attempt to hold down wage increases. The pound was devalued in 1967 and again in 1972 in an attempt to hold back real wages and to increase the profitability (competitiveness) of British products. But workers responded to the slow growth of their real incomes after devaluation of 1967 by the wage explosion since 1970. The Industrial Relations Act was introduced to break the organized power of the working class but was greeted in 1972 by the largest number of days lost through strikes since the general strike of 1926. Finally, incomes policy is now aimed at increasing profitability. For there is talk in the Phase 2 proposals of profit margins being limited to the average of the best two out of the last five years. Since profitability hardly increased since 1970, despite all the efforts I have described, this would allow a substantial increase in the profit share (from about 13 per cent to 15.5 per cent).

There is little recognition among union leaders that working-class demands are implicitly challenging the capitalist system in Britain. Most place great hopes in the return of a Labor government pledged to pursue a more expansionary and fairer policy. But they ignore the fact that such a government, from its ideological basis of making capitalism work, will again be forced to attack the working class. Without the development of a revolutionary leadership, which understands the necessity for smashing capitalism rather than hoping to peacefully transform it, the way is opened for the working class, despite its strength, to be defeated by a capitalist class which will move towards fascist methods.

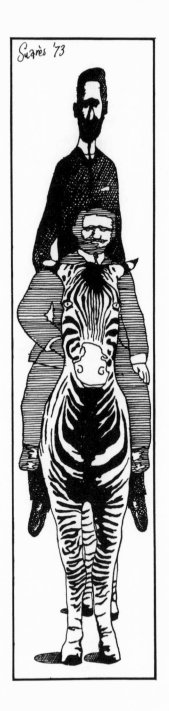

DAVID ROCKEFELLER
The Essential Quest for the Middle Way

Profits, says David Rockefeller, chairman of the Chase Manhattan Bank, make the capitalistic system spin: they enable business to develop new products, carry on research, innovate, increase productivity, and deliver the goods. But that's not the whole story, he contends: capitalism is a highly flexible and evolutionary concept—not a sitting duck for its critics, but a moving target—within which not only economic objectives but social and personal needs can be fulfilled.

Business, he believes, must try to live up to its social responsibilities, but it shares those responsibilities with government, labor, nonprofit groups, and the rest of the community. He suggests that the power of business to solve all sorts of problems is exaggerated: such problems as pollution, crime, housing, employment, and energy needs will require joint efforts for their solution and greater business, government, and social involvement in long-range planning. He calls this approach an American "middle way."

Rockefeller's concept does not appear essentially statist but rather a contemporary version of the classic liberal and pluralist society, held together by a system of rights and duties which at any given time represents "a slightly antiquated formulation of the balance of power among the active interests in the community," as Walter Lippmann once said. No single power element can control the nation on the full range of issues that face it; the diffusion of power is essential to the preservation of freedom. Problems come to public opinion only

*irregularly and on appeal; even public opinion must not become too
powerful, or it can become tyrannical.*

*Business executives are highly sensitive to the pressures of other
groups, and particularly to the powers of government, these days.
They do not feel that they are in control; rather, they feel controlled.
As one businessman remarked to me, "We can't even control the
mess in our backyards."*

Capitalism today, as frequently in the past, is the object of
strident criticism. Indeed, the variety of divergent sins placed
upon its shoulders is truly remarkable: inequitable wealth, pollution, and consumer deception are the most common accusations.

With the word "capitalism" carrying so many overtones, it is
small wonder that capitalist and anticapitalist alike often find
themselves confused. Perhaps this is because both attackers and
defenders are trying too hard to transform a highly evolutionary
and flexible concept into a sitting duck.

Extreme interpretations have two major drawbacks. They
miss the true nature of capitalism, and they increase the difficulty
of implementing necessary improvements. While we all crave
simple and consistent concepts, capitalism constantly resists rigid
classification. The challenge I see is to regard the lack of ideological purity in our system as a positive opportunity rather than
as a negative problem. Indeed, the greatest strength of capitalism
is probably its adaptability. Having the virtue of relative freedom, it is able to respond to changing circumstances more
readily than tightly controlled systems—especially in an economy
as large and complex as that of the United States.

This responsiveness in turn helps create high levels of productivity and income. It also offers in its diversity unique opportunities for economic growth, social progress, and personal

freedom and fulfillment. Moreover, the capacity of this flexible system to deal relatively quickly with new problems is of particular importance when we look to the future.

Keeping capitalism up to date will amply challenge this innate flexibility in the years ahead. It is a matter of particular urgency that we find means to overcome the alienation perceived by many people between our economic progress and the attainment of our other social goals. Failure to bridge this gap and understand the deep-seated virtues of capitalism may lead to public policies that make it impossible to generate the profits necessary to make the system work. Profits play a basic role in fueling the developing of new productive resources, spurring technological innovation, and encouraging the more efficient and economical delivery of goods and services.

On the other hand, if American capitalism is to maintain and increase its vitality, it must do a better job of integrating its economic and social functions. Toward this end I would offer three suggestions.

First, corporations must develop more effective tools for measuring the social, as well as economic, costs and benefits of their actions. A broadly acceptable format for detailed social accounting is probably a distant goal, yet there is much that can be done now. Social objectives can be formally incorporated into regular business planning. Managers can be evaluated, in part, on the social productivity. Corporate expertise in cost-benefit analysis can be applied on a test basis to socially related projects.

Whatever the methods, it is vital that social accountability become an integral part of corporate conduct, rather than a philanthropic add-on. Only in that way will the economic development of the private sector move forward within an acceptable framework of public purpose. Only in that way will corporations assure the healthy social climate vital to their own future economic prosperity.

Second, businessmen must take the initiative to spell out more clearly and positively the longer-range economic and technical implications of current proposals for social problem-solving.

Too often, in the view of businessmen, critics seem simply to proclaim goals as solutions without taking into account the necessary processes, resources, and economic dislocations. Critics of business, on the other hand, frequently brand those who point to the costs of social progress as mossbacks. Neither group is exclusively correct. It is rarely acknowledged by both sides that very real problems exist and that without hard and practical evaluations of the relative costs and benefits we can never develop approaches that are the most desirable to society as a whole. The resulting conflict hardly leads to a constructive relationship.

If we are to come up with feasible and effective programs, we must do much more to develop cooperative undertakings that bring the enormously diverse talents of the business community to bear on the problems of our society. Problems such as pollution abatement, provision of good housing, and the need to supply adequate sources of energy are exceedingly complex and require concerted and dedicated action. Unless business takes a leadership role in creating workable solutions, it will only suffer with its environment. It will also abdicate to government and others much of its potential for a more positive position in our society.

Finally, we must press forward on the national level to create broader and more viable long-range goals, to assess what business can and cannot do to meet those goals, and to set more comprehensive strategies to combine the strengths of public and private resources.

98

Problem-solving in America has a tendency to be short-lived —yesterday civil rights and education, today pollution, tomorrow crime, and so on. We take issues in isolation, look for panaceas, get discouraged, and move to something new. Rarely do we carefully examine the complex interactions of our society, calculate the necessary trade-offs, and assign the required resources on a sustained basis. Obtaining even vague consensus on goals is not easy, and many noble attempts have faltered. And yet, government, business, private citizens, and the academic community must strive to come up with mutually agreeable long-range objectives.

At the same time we must also strengthen our general understanding of who is responsible for what. Listening to some commentators, you would think business could solve all problems, while others suggest that government is the only hope. The truth is somewhere in between, with many areas, such as environment or employment or housing, requiring joint efforts. Family assistance and education, on the other hand, are primarily public problems, though some joint efforts to improve administration have been very fruitful. If government, business, labor, and nonprofit groups could sharpen their sense of respective resources and responsibility, progress could be much faster.

Making social responsibility an integral part of corporate planning, realistically evaluating the necessary resources for social problem-solving, and fostering a clearer sense of national goals and the appropriate distribution of responsibility are, of course, not solutions in themselves to the challenges we face. Combined with the inherent strength and flexibility of capitalism, however, endeavors toward these ends will help us continue to move toward our common objectives of economic viability, social progress, and personal fulfillment.

Suarès '73

WASSILY LEONTIEF
Sails and Rudders, Ship of State

Wassily Leontief, professor of economics at Harvard University and 1973 winner of the Nobel Prize in economic science, shares with David Rockefeller the view that the United States needs more long-range economic planning. Leontief, inventor of the input-output system of economic analysis that is widely used in socialist and communist countries as a tool for economic planning, is no collectivist. He thinks it is possible to direct the powerful American economy primarily through the tax system, public subsidies, antipollution regulations, and so forth, rather than through collective ownership and management.

What is most important for the United States now, he suggests, is not how fast it goes but where it goes. The American society has been hell-bent for maximum speed in increasing output while tolerating large pockets of poverty, social inequality, poor public services, limited recreation facilities, an inefficient and foul transportation system, poor public health, a horrible prison system, growing crime rates, and other manifestations of social neglect that make it something less than the envy of the world. And the Nixon administration, he contends, is making all this worse.

A naïve, simplistic view of the internal social struggles shaping the emergence of a small Asiatic country from its colonial past caused the United States to pay a colossal price in treasure, human lives, and moral standing throughout the civilized world. Now an equally simplistic view of conflicting forces that constantly shape and reshape our own society prompts the Nixon administration to embark on a program of domestic policies for which this country will have to pay a still higher price in diminished material well-being, retarded social progress, and waning self-respect.

Curtailment of support for public housing, trimming of government programs in various fields of health care, training, and education, restraining of decisive action in the combat against environmental disruption, and abandonment of any thought of a tax reform designed to reduce the inequality of income distribution are only a few examples of policies whose obvious purpose is to slow down, to arrest, or even to roll back public action designed to meet the growing challenges that threaten our society.

References to the moral virtues of self-reliance and self-help, to the efficacy of private enterprise, and the blessings of untrammeled competition leave no doubt that at the bottom of all this lies the profound belief that most social and economic problems would be solved or simply vanish if ITT and a small homesteader in the Ozarks, a Puerto Rican family occupying a two-room cold-water flat in Harlem, and the owner of a duplex luxury apartment on East End Avenue were simply encouraged to defend and promote their separate interests by any and all means available to each one of them. Such a belief can be based only on a profound misunderstanding of the system in which all of us live and of the forces that keep it moving.

The pursuit of private economic gains is certainly the mighty power source that propels the American economy forward. Under our system of free enterprise the profit motive in particular promotes and safeguards its unequaled technical and managerial efficiency. This is the wind that keeps the vessel moving.

But to keep it on a chosen course we have to use a rudder. The steering apparatus consists of taxes, subsidies, antipollution regulations, and other measures of governmental economic policies. There are, of course, those who say that we should simply hoist the sails and let the vessel go before the wind in whatever direction the wind happens to be blowing. This type of navigation is bound to bring the ship off its course and land it on the rocks, and the stronger the wind the greater the peril.

In some socialist countries, on the other hand, they have taken down the sails and thus lost the driving power of the profit motive. No wonder the rudder has lost its steering power too. Some of these economies are cautiously returning to sail power; others still try to propel themselves by planned paddling in the hope that soon some new kind of engine will be invented, one that can drive an economy without reliance on the trade winds of material incentive.

Private enterprise made this country the most prosperous in the world, and our economy will, of course, rely on it as its main driving force for a long time to come. But to keep on the right course we certainly have to use the rudder and, by all indications, the government will have to lean on it more heavily in the future than it did in the past.

This country has for too long been "blown" by uncontrolled profit motive in the direction of increasing economic maladjustment and growing social disruption. The time has come to correct its course by tacking (the art of sailing a vessel in a direction different from that in which the wind is blowing). There can be

103

hardly any doubt that the use of the rudder is bound to cut the speed of the economy, as it does of a vessel on the water. Subsidized public housing may be managed less efficiently than cooperative luxury apartment buildings; a ton of coal scooped from an open pit certainly costs less than coal mined underground; a radical tax reform that would reduce the burden carried by lower incomes and take a bigger bite off the top might, from what we know, cut somewhat the total volume of private savings and investment and thus tend to lower the rate of economic growth. But does this mean that public housing should be liquidated, restrictions on strip mining weakened, and the plans for a major tax reform dropped? Not at all.

Only those who have little faith in the driving force of American private enterprise can argue that it will simply falter when confronted with determined public action—action designed to prevent this force from propelling the country toward economic and social maladjustment. Past experience justifies the hope that the profit motive can be effectively harnessed to advance the country on a course toward solid economic balance and greater social justice.

KENNETH J. ARROW
Capitalism, for Better or Worse

Karl Marx and Friedrich Engels saw history as full of dialectical processes—inner contradictions and conflicts, whose resolution inexorably served as the driving force of economic and social progress. The class struggle was the prime example of this dialectical movement, through which ruling classes were continuously opposed and eventually overthrown by the classes they had dominated; history would, in effect, come to an end with the achievement of the classless society.

In the following essay Kenneth J. Arrow, professor of economics at Harvard and 1972 Nobel laureate in economics, examines six fundamental contradictions of capitalism, not all of them put forward by Marxists, and concludes that they need not be fatal, at least in the foreseeable future. Indeed, capitalism may be strengthened for resolving them.

There is little warrant for the belief that we know the laws of history well enough to make projections of any great reliability. Most of the turning points of history, great and small, were surprises to both their participants and the analysts of the day, whatever their doctrine.

That the capitalist system excels at productive efficiency is not

105

to be denied. In the United States, Western Europe, and Japan, at least, the rate of increase in efficiency is much higher now than it was when the authors of the Communist Manifesto included a fulsome panegyric on the productive accomplishments of the bourgeoisie. But no social institution has ever felt justified solely by material product. Moreover, the inequalities in the distribution of this material wealth and in the power and control over the activities by which it is created constitute a steady indictment.

This indictment has, among several different groups of social analysts, taken the empirical form of asserting that the development of capitalism has given rise to "contradictions" that imply its eventual extinction as a matter of historical law. As I have said, I do not believe us capable of discerning inevitable contradictions and, in any case, capitalism has survived long enough in advanced countries to show that the contradictions can hardly be fatal, though they may have been avoided only by the development of new institutions, such as labor unions and government intervention.

It is still useful to list some six of the leading proposed contradictions, for they do all point to real problems for social policy and criticism. No doubt the idea of a contradiction in the capitalist system is Marxian in origin, but some of the following contradictions have been put forward by non-Marxists only and some by both sides.

1. *Ideological weakness.* Capitalism relies for its operation on selfish motives. Its prized efficiency depends on the greed of the owners and managers of firms, on their desire for increasing profits. Further, the success of capitalism depends on careful calculation, on a nice balancing of costs and benefits. The reliance on selfishness is defended as a realistic evaluation of human

motivations. But neither selfishness nor calculation are goals for which men are willing to make deep commitments. It is a fear of many conservative thinkers, the late Joseph Schumpeter being perhaps the best known and most thoroughgoing and Irving Kristol being the latest, that the ideological commitment to capitalism is too weak to resist the idealistic appeal of socialism or similar doctrines, which promise a daily contribution to the common good.

2. *Alienation.* A closely related critical theme holds that capitalism, with its emphasis on the impersonal-exchange relationship, leads to destruction of personal and communal relations. If these are fundamental needs of mankind, then alienation ultimately undermines the social relations that define the capitalist system itself. This thesis, put forward vigorously by conservative and romantic thinkers of the early nineteenth century, was adopted by Marx, but with an added characteristic element: the worker is alienated from the product of his labor, his work becomes merely a means to income, not the satisfaction of a need to be productive. The human-relations movement in industry illustrates how the same critique can be put to defend and improve personal hierarchical relations in industry.

3. *Increasing concentration.* Marx and many others have argued that competition and technological development force a growing concentration of economic power into fewer and fewer hands. Among other alleged consequences: the size of the class that benefits from capitalism would be steadily shrinking, and therefore the system would be more vulnerable, and the transition to a centrally controlled socialist economy would be made easier.

The actual development has revealed some factors that modify these effects. The hypothesis of growing concentration and the two consequences just drawn were based on observations in the industrial sector of the economy. But the degree of concentration in the industrial sector seems to have reached a stable level and has not changed greatly in fifty years or more; the exercise of control in giant firms itself requires an increasingly large fraction of the employees, who become identified in some measure with the directing groups; and the proportion of employment in the industrial sector is decreasing, as rising incomes cause more expenditure on services, which tend to be operated by smaller firms.

4. *Working-class solidarity.* The grouping of workers for effective production, as in factories, reinforces the sense of their common position as against the employers. The sense of solidarity gave strength to the tendency to unionization and, in Europe, to the socialist and syndicalist movements. The intensity of feeling in these movements, exemplified in the sit-down strikes in the United States during the late thirties, certainly appeared to justify the notion of intense class conflict.

In fact, several factors have mitigated the thrust of working-class solidarity: the conflict between unions and employers has become institutionalized and legitimized wherever unions have become strong enough to reach a level of security; not only are the economic conflicts fought out in ways that pose no threat to the social order, but politically organized labor plays a relatively more conservative role than in the past.

There is, however, one unresolved strain in labor relations which has come to surprise us: the determination of wages and working conditions in the public sector. In recent years we have moved to unions and strikes in this region. We clearly have not come to an institutional equilibrium here; laws against strikes are

109

not enforced, not even in the case of police, where striking has some especially severe consequences. Labor relations in privately owned public utilities pose some of the same special problems. This development can hardly be called a contradiction of capitalism, to be sure.

5. *Unemployment.* Over the last hundred and fifty years by far the most serious criticism of, and threat to, the capitalist economic system has been the recurring cycles of unemployment. Here was a clear malfunctioning of the system itself, not attributable to external causes imposing misery on its victims. Further, not only was it to be expected that insecurity and patently unnecessary poverty would create resentment and violent antagonism on the part of the working class, but also each depression was accompanied by a destruction of profits, the lifeblood and raison d'être of the capitalist system. It seemed a reasonable extrapolation to foresee a collápse of the system, both economical and political. But no such collapse occurred. Not even the Great Depression caused a serious question to be raised, except perhaps in the special case of Germany. Perhaps the clearly evident growth in the real incomes of all members of the society more than compensated for the recurrent economic disasters.

The new economic ideas of Keynes and his disciples have been translated into policy with almost unprecedented speed. The idea that the state, through its decisions to spend, tax, and regulate the supply of money, could reduce unemployment to levels far lower than those in the depths of previous depressions was accepted among both economists and political leaders and has shown itself to work in practice with great success. In every advanced country the post–World War II economic record is like that of a new economy. Sophisticated radical economists, such as Paul Baran and Paul Sweezy, quickly recognized that the Keynes-

110

ian solution would work but argued that in a capitalist system the government could spend enough to insure full employment only on socially wasteful and even destructive ends, such as war and preparations for war. Socially constructive spending would necessarily compete with and eventually undermine the private sector. The example of Japan suggests some reason to doubt this argument, though the Japanese circumstances are somewhat special. At home over the last decade it has been found possible to achieve a much higher level of government spending on social purposes and to decrease defense expenditures at least relatively. We do have higher unemployment rates than are desirable, but that is because of inflationary fears rather than a shortage of ways to spend money. There is little reason, therefore, to accept the Baran-Sweezy variation of the unemployment contradiction though perhaps it is too soon to regard it as definitely controverted.

6. *Inflation*. There appears to be this element of truth in the idea of a contradiction: the resolution of any problem always creates a new problem. From the beginning of the Keynesian era the fear has been expressed that vigorous full-employment policies will lead to inflation. Standard economic theory has been built in large measure about the idea of equilibrium, that an exact balancing of supply and demand on all markets, including the labor market, will lead to steady prices, while an excess of supply leads to a downward pressure. Thus, unemployment ought to lead to wage declines; they manifestly have not done so in recent years. The coexistence of inflation and unemployment is thus an intellectual riddle and an uncomfortable fact.

But in my judgment the contradiction here hardly compares with some of the others to which capitalism has adapted.

First of all, the rates of inflation with which we have had to

111

contend impose no insuperable problem or even major difficulty to the operation of the economic system, nothing comparable to the major depressions of the past. Individuals will learn, and have learned, to deal with inflation, making their plans to take expected inflation into account. The economic system and the government will create and are creating methods of mitigating the effects, such as variable-annuity plans and cost-of-living clauses in savings bonds. What the future will bring is of course a matter of conjecture. Some analysts feel that inflation will inevitably accelerate, but others will note that in the past peacetime inflations have tapered off. The present rates are historically high but not totally unprecedented; it appears from the record that even in peacetime, over the period 1897–1902, prices rose more rapidly than they have in the last five years.

Second, we may have some reasonable hope that economic research and experimentation in policymaking, between them, will evolve more sophisticated means of managing the overall economy. Research into monetary economics is at an unprecedented level of activity, and better and more abundant data are available than ever before. With the variety of policy instruments now available and better understood, I think it most likely that the reconciliation of full employment and price stability can be significantly improved in the future.

We find that capitalism, like any very complex system, contains within itself contradictory tendencies, but there is no reason to suppose they are fatal, at least in the foreseeable future. We do find implied in these contradictions some social tasks: the completion of the tasks involved in the achievement of macroeconomic stability, the redistribution of income and power to improve the sense of justice in the arrangements of society, by which I mean the inseparable elements of the liberty and equality of individuals, and, perhaps hardest, the increase in the sense of individual and local control over one's destiny in the workplace and the small society. These aims are mutually reinforcing, not competitive.

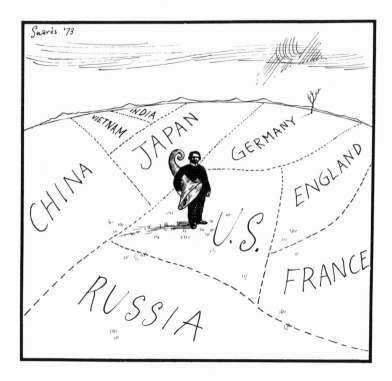

PAUL A. SAMUELSON
Taking Stock of War

One of the fundamental radical charges against the capitalist system is that it tends to erupt in periodic wars—wars among capitalist powers competing for markets, imperialist wars among capitalist nations seeking resources and high profits in the poor and backward countries, capitalist wars generated by unemployment at home and the political convenience of massive military expenditures as a means of regaining prosperity.

Paul A. Samuelson, professor of economics at the Massachusetts Institute of Technology, who in 1970 became the first American to win the Nobel Prize in economics, contends that the Marxist critics were once right to worry about the tendency of the capitalist system to fall periodically into depression and mass unemployment, which war could conveniently arrest, but that since the Keynesian revolution in economics governments could sustain full employment by rationally determined spending, tax, and monetary policies without the necessity of bloody war; wars can only aggravate the current problem of cost-push inflation and stagnation. Yet Samuelson is no easy optimist about the likely disappearance of wars; he suggests a number of other reasons for not sleeping too soundly.

115

Three questions deserve hard-headed and unflinching investigation.

1. Are great, or little, wars inevitable because of the capitalist class's pursuit of profits? If not inevitable, are wars nevertheless more likely than under noncapitalist regimes (socialism, feudalism, the modern mixed economy)?

2. Are there particular groups of capitalists who profit from war—merchants of death in the form of munitions makers and, more generally, an entrenched and powerful military-industrial complex? Are there imperialistic investors abroad, whose pecuniary interests are furthered or preserved by war? Is it the lobbying and political power of such interests that contribute importantly to the occurrence and duration of great and little wars?

3. Leaving aside the parochial interests of the plutocratic or property-owning classes, is it the case that all the citizens of a market economy have a recognized or covert interest in war—for the reasons, first, that capitalism must break down in depression if it does not find imperialistic ventures that spend money and destroy surplus goods, and, second, that high living standards of the few advanced nations can be maintained only by exploitation of the teeming billions who live in the impoverished, underdeveloped nations?

To answer these questions, begin with the writings of ideologues: defenders of nineteenth-century capitalism (Adam Smith's followers, Hayek, Milton Friedman, Barry Goldwater, your great-uncle), revolutionary critics of Victorian capitalism (Karl Marx and Friedrich Engels, Rosa Luxemburg and V. I. Lenin, Paul Sweezy and Paul Baran, Jack Gurley and Sam Bowles, your freshman brother at Yale).

You find your work has just begun. One sweeping, monistic

explanation cancels out another. Alas, there is no substitute for tedious analysis of historical experience, unsparing analysis of what makes the macroeconomics of the mixed economy tick, and sophisticated insight into the checks-and-balances of realistic power politics.

Let's begin by answering a couple of the easy questions. Of course, particular groups benefit from war. Generals, for one (and they both antedate the market system and postdate it). Sergeants, for another. Assembly-line workers on bombers, their spouses, their unions, their congressmen. And let's not forget the corporations whose activities are specialized to the defense industry.

But little or nothing follows from this. Somebody stands to benefit from every dollar of the gross national product. The plowshare industry stands to gain from peace, just as the sword industry gains from war. ITT has so well hedged a portfolio that only God knows—certainly Harold Geneen doesn't—where its pocketbook interests lie.

"Wait a minute," you will say. "Aren't you forgetting that war expenditures may be an add-on to gross national product—the something extra that permits underconsuming capitalism to get rid of its unemployment and its declining rate of profit?"

No. I am simply remembering that this is 1973, not 1903 or 1933. We are almost forty years into the Age of Keynes. I believe that Luxemburg and Lenin (and Hobson and Alvin Hansen) were right to worry about the sustainability of full employment in William McKinley's balanced-budget laissez-faire. However, not a single mixed economy has had any problem these last thirty years with chronic insufficiency of purchasing power. (Go down the list: the United States, Britain, France, Japan, Germany, little Belgium.)

117

Nor in the century to come—1973–2073—will the ancient scourge of intermittent-shortage-of-purchasing power reoccur in the old form.

("What about recession and stagflation, professor? Don't deny they still happen!" Of course they do. And in 1983 or 2013 they may still occur to plague the mixed economy. But Sweezy and Bowles know what Lenin and Luxemburg couldn't know—that the disease of cost-push inflation which is involved in stagflation has nought to do with insufficiency of domestic markets, and cold- or hot-war escapades can do nothing to make it better.)

After the few easy answers of somebody-gains-somebody-loses-from-war and wars-no-longer-needed-to-prime-the pump we are left with hard questions.

1. A World War III between Russia and China, two noncapitalistic countries, is as likely as between any two market economies and as likely as a war between the United States and either Russia or China or both of them.

2. The fact that the mixed economies of North America, Western Europe, and elsewhere will not willingly go through a Communist revolution or the socialist societies of Eastern Europe and Asia will not willingly go through a counterrevolution or takeover, could produce acute or chronic warfare in the future. In this sense "capitalism-plus-Communism" might be deemed potential causes of war.

3. Revolution and insurrection cannot always be distinguished from war. The fact that wealth and power are unequally distributed, within nations and between nations, must be regarded as a potential cause of conflict and war.

4. Adam Smith's "invisible hand of self-interest" leads you to pick the best growth stock, the best hi-fi, and to vote for Richard Nixon. That same hand will lead other people to take over in the

118

future foreign copper mines and oil concessions. And who is to say that the invisible hand which leads people to the ballot box will not someday lead them also to the barricades and the front-line trenches?

A.   B.   C.

PAUL M. SWEEZY
Capitalism, for Worse

Paul M. Sweezy, a Marxist economist who once taught at Harvard and is now coeditor of Monthly Review, *takes sharp issue with the contention of Arrow and Samuelson that the Keynesian revolution has provided capitalist nations with the means or will to prevent heavy unemployment. He contends that the facts of open and disguised unemployment in the United States contradict this proposition.*

He maintains that the historic tendency of capitalist production to outrun the system's power to consume, is deeper and more pervasive today than in Marx's time and that this inherent "contradiction" of the system still generates wars as a means of sustaining prosperity. He contends that capitalist nations such as the Federal Republic of Germany and Japan, which have not engaged in war since their devastation in World War II, have prospered in the postwar era by living off the stimulus provided by American military activities. He fears that the continuation of the capitalist system threatens continuous global violence and the very existence of mankind.

With few exceptions the economists of the capitalist countries, liberal and conservative alike, are agreed that in the nearly four decades since the publication of Keynes's *General Theory of Employment, Interest, and Money* governments have been in possession of, and have successfully utilized, the means of controlling

121

the level of economic activity and preventing the occurrence of serious depressions. To quote Harvard's economist Kenneth J. Arrow above, Nobel Prize winner,

The new economic ideas of Keynes and his disciples have been translated into policy with almost unprecedented speed. The idea that the state, through its decisions to spend, tax, and regulate the supply of money, could reduce unemployment to levels far lower than those in the depths of previous depressions was accepted among both economists and political leaders and has shown itself to work in practice with great success. In every advanced country the post World War II record is like that of a new economy.

Let us look for a moment at the United States record (I will return to the others later on). It is true that since World War II there have been no depressions comparable to that of the nineteen-thirties. But is this because economists and political leaders have put their heads together and decided upon appropriate spending, tax, and monetary policies to head one off every time it threatened? Or is it because there has been a tremendous increase in the general level of government spending, armaments and war playing by far the largest part? (I presume that neither the economists nor the political leaders would wish to claim that the military spending is merely the form taken by Keynesian ideas when put into practice.)

To these questions our economist friends would probably reply that, although for overriding political or foreign-policy reasons the requisite amount of government spending has in fact been for military purposes, if this had not been the case it would have been possible to spend a great deal more for welfare objectives, with much the same economic results. In their eyes the theory of the controllability of the level of economic activity is therefore vindicated, regardless of what the money is spent on.

If this were really so, however, would we not expect that the controllers, helped by the large military budget, would have had an easy time maintaining a reasonably satisfactory level of economic activity throughout the postwar period? Surely with 20 per cent or more of the American people living below the officially defined poverty line and with such projects as decent low-cost housing, pollution control, and mass transportation crying out for vastly increased public outlays, there has never been any lack of worthy purposes for the controllers to turn their attention to. And yet it is a notorious fact that even in boom times, as at the time of writing in June 1973, officially counted unemployment amounts to 5 per cent or more of the labor force. Taking facts like this into account, one could be pardoned for suspecting that the whole "controllability" idea is a myth and that the military budget is after all the only rational explanation of the relatively favorable (relative to the nineteen-thirties) economic record of the postwar period.

In order to test this hypothesis, my colleague Harry Magdoff and I conducted an "experiment."[1] Using commonsense and generally conservative estimating methods, we calculated for the year 1970 the number of workers who were either unemployed or directly and indirectly dependent on military spending. We then added these figures and compared the result with the number of unemployed in 1938. (It should be noted that both 1970 and 1938 were years of recession following a long period of cyclical upswing and should therefore be fairly comparable.)

The first problem was to get an estimate of real, as distinct from officially counted, unemployment, since everyone familiar with the subject knows that there is a large discrepancy.[2] Work-

[1] Reported in detail in "Economic Stagnation and the Stagnation of Economics," *Monthly Review,* April 1971.

[2] See, for example, the article on unemployment entitled "6 Pct. Is Only the Tip of the Iceberg" by A. H. Raskin in *The New York Times,* "Review of the Week" section, June 25, 1972.

ing from official data on labor-force participation rates, which were steadily declining for male workers during most of the nineteen-fifties and nineteen-sixties, and making an adjustment for involuntary part-time workers, we concluded that a conservative estimate of real unemployment was 8.1 million (9.4 per cent of what would have been the labor force if jobs had been available). To this we added those in the armed forces (2.9 million), civilian employees of the Defense Department (1.2 million), those employed in producing goods for the Defense Department (3 million), and those employed because of what economists call the multiplier effect, or workers employed in satisfying the demand generated by the incomes of those directly employed by the military budget (7.1 million). These items total 22.3 million. This is just over 25 per cent of the 1970 labor force adjusted to include those not officially counted as unemployed.

This compares with an official unemployment figure of 19.0 per cent in 1938. However, if we make adjustments for hidden unemployment at that time and add to the expanded total the relatively small number of defense-related employed, we would probably come up with a figure somewhere around 30 per cent to compare with the 25 per cent in 1970. All of which leads to the conclusion that, apart from military spending, things were a bit better in 1970 than in 1938. But not much, and certainly nowhere near enough to sustain the thesis that the economists and politicians are in effective control of the economy.

If my Keynesian friends wish to dispute these facts or estimates, I would be happy to hear from them. I confess, however, that I do not expect to. They like to talk about the record, but they are shy about subjecting it to a concrete historical analysis. In this connection it is worth noting, if only in passing, that they have not yet come up with a coherent theory of the Great Depression and why it was so much worse than any previous capitalist depression. Need I add that without such a theory it is quite impossible to provide any rational analysis of what might have happened in the postwar period in the absence of vastly expanded military spending?

At this point the Keynesians, with remarkable unanimity, shift their ground. What about the other advanced capitalist countries, they ask, and especially Germany and Japan, the two with the best growth and employment records and the lowest levels of military spending?

It is impossible to answer this question adequately in a brief essay, especially since, to the best of my knowledge, no one, and least of all the Keynesians, has made a serious effort to do so. I can therefore only indicate the general lines along which I believe an attempt at an answer should proceed.

Most fundamental here is the fact, too often forgotten by social scientists, each working in his or her narrow specialty, that capitalism is a global system and not a collection of separate national economies. What happens in any part of the system affects to some extent what happens in all the others; and if the part in question happens to be by far the largest in the system, as is the case of the United States in world capitalism, the effect on some or all of the other parts is likely to be large and even decisive. The question, then, is to what extent the performance of the world capitalist economy, and especially the economies of Germany and Japan, has been determined by the relative prosperity of the United States during this period.

It is, I believe, beyond dispute that both the German and the Japanese economic "miracles" were launched in the boom that accompanied the Korean War, as a direct result, that is, of United

125

States military spending and involvement. For the case of Germany, Heinz Abosch has written: "For the West German economy, the Korean War proved to be a remarkable stimulant: while the big industrial powers had to step up the production of armaments, Germany, still subject to the restrictions of the Potsdam Agreement, was able to increase her entire industrial output, thanks to the orders that poured in from all sides. As Professor Henry Wallich remarks, 'It was sparks from the Korean War that set German exports alight.' "[3] What was true for Germany was even more so for Japan, which was the rear staging area for United States forces fighting in Korea and a direct recipient of large military orders. "In terms of the growth situation," writes Professor Tsuru, "the Korean conflict and the subsequent maintenance of 'special procurement' demand was a distinct boon."[4]

Of course it would not be possible to establish so close a continuing dependence of the German and Japanese economies on United States military spending. The booms touched off by Korea had much else to feed on: repair of war damage, renovation of capital equipment and, perhaps most important, a veritable binge of "automobilization" similar to that which had sustained the United States economy in the twenties. But continuing strong demand for German and Japanese exports remained a sine qua non of the prosperity of these countries, and it is difficult to believe that this export demand would have held up if the United States economy had once again sunk into a condition of low-level stagnation such as prevailed in the thirties. It is well to

---

[3] Heinz Abosch, *The Menace of the Miracle* (New York, 1963), p. 79.

[4] Shigeto Tsuru, *Essays in Economic Development,* Economic Research Series No. 9 (Tokyo, 1968), p. 168. "Special Procurement" was the name given to U.S. purchases for military and related purposes. According to Professor Tsuru's figures (pp. 156–157), this item averaged 34.2 per cent of Japan's total receipts from foreign sales of goods and services in the years 1951–1953.

remember that in that earlier period it was only military spending, first in Japan and Germany and only later in the United States, which pulled the capitalist world out of the Great Depression. In the postwar period I would argue that it has been military spending (plus other similarly motivated outlays, such as economic subsidies to puppet and client states), so far largely but by no means exclusively centered in the United States, which has prevented the capitalist world from sinking into a new Great Depression. As an historical interpretation of these strife-ridden decades, I submit that this makes vastly more sense than the notion that the postwar performance of world capitalism has been the brainchild of economists aided and abetted by wise political leaders. Economists may like to think that they are powerful, and political leaders that they are wise. But the sad truth is that there is precious little evidence to support these amiable conceits. True, they play a role, but not the one they think they play or would like to play; rather, their role is that of instruments and agents of elemental forces generated by a blind and self-contradictory economic system that no one can control.

The real question to which economists ought to address themselves, but consistently refuse to do so, is why capitalism in the twentieth century has such a powerful tendency to stagnation that it requires increasingly massive forms of public and private waste to keep itself going at all. (As every reasonably sensitive observer of contemporary capitalism knows, military spending is only the leading species of a large genus.) Basically, the reason was stated by Marx with both eloquence and clarity more than a hundred years ago when he wrote: *"The real barrier of capitalist production is capital itself.* It is the fact that capital and its self-expansion appear as the starting and closing point, as the motive and aim of production, that production is merely production for

127

capital and not vice versa, the means of production merely means for an ever-expanding system of the life process for the benefit of the *society* of producers."[5] To put the point in another way, as long as the driving forces of production are profit and the expansion of profit-making enterprises, and as long as the incomes of working people are held down precisely to make possible an increase in profits and a more rapid expansion of enterprises, so long will the growth of society's power to produce tend to outstrip its power to consume. And if this contradiction is deeper and more pervasive today than it was in Marx's time, the reason is that in the intervening period the process of concentration and centralization of capital—which he recognized as inevitable features of capitalist development—has gone so far that dominant monopolies today have the power not only to exploit their own workers but all other strata of society as well, thus expanding the gap between wealth at one pole and poverty at the other, at the very time that there is or soon could be ample productive power to provide everyone, without exception, with the means to a decent human livelihood.

Under these circumstances economists have taken upon themselves the task of hiding the facts, of making the uncontrollable appear under control, of rationalizing a system that condemns hundreds of millions of people to lives of despair and starvation and that, through its unrestrained profligacy and violence, threatens the very continuation of life on earth. It is not a task I envy them.

[5] Karl Marx, *Capital*, Vol. 3, p. 293. Italics in the original.

GABRIEL KOLKO
A War from Time to Time

As a New Left "revisionist," Gabriel Kolko, professor of history at York University in Toronto, does not have a neat theory of the relationship between capitalism and war. He suggests that it is necessary to weigh a number of radical propositions: that economic stagnation at home causes capitalist nations to go on military adventures abroad, that the military-industrial complex (seeking orders, money, jobs, power) wins widespread national support for an aggressive United States foreign policy, that rich nations need to exploit poor nations for their raw materials, that capitalists fear genuine social revolutions in the Third World, that trade, monetary, and energy rivalries will make the capitalist powers fight among themselves and so on.

But less arguable than the theories of war and capitalism, he contends, is the fact of war. His deep anxiety, in the wake of what he calls the "Indochina debacle," is that however complex or mysterious the inner process, capitalism will continue to generate crises and wars —which will finally cause capitalism itself to collapse.

The way Americans define the causes of the Indochina debacle will determine whether they shall be intellectually prepared to anticipate future crises. Conventional wisdom still attributes America's role in Vietnam to accidents or bureaucratic myopia,

thereby slighting the real meaning of the consistency of American interventions in the Third World in suppressing radical forces and preserving semicolonial societies.

Vietnam was an "accident" along a much older, intrinsically dangerous route only insofar as Washington's goals there far exceeded its power to attain them, and it eventually became profoundly dysfunctional to the United States' global priorities and needs. But to divorce Vietnam and numerous interventions from the specific goals of American capitalism in the world, assuming that the needs and value of capitalism are irrelevant to the range of policy options decision-makers consider, is sanctioned ideology but poor history and debilitating to our capacity to anticipate our future.

War, from preparations through aftermath, is the central element in defining the essential quality of capitalist societies as well as their relative powers throughout this century, and it has also become the main catalyst to revolutionary movements and changes in vast areas. If it temporarily sustains prosperity or saves weakened ruling groups, in the longer run, especially for defeated nations, war exacerbates latent domestic social tensions.

While the outcome of this process is not necessarily revolution on the left, and just as often leads to counterrevolution or reaction, it increases disorder within a nation and diminishes its ability to compete economically with other capitalist states. United States economic supremacy until 1962 was to some critical degree based on the consequences of Europe's two major internecine wars, while America avoided protracted, large-scale combat. Yet for the past decade the reverse has been true, Europe and Japan today being relatively far stronger thereby.

Protracted war imposes a debilitating political context on the purely economic aspects of capitalist power, which then seriously

131

dilutes, or even eliminates, whatever domestic equilibrium efforts at economic or social control make possible. Economic compulsions, in turn, constrict the range of international options policymakers may consider. They cannot ignore stagnation due to underconsumption at home, the need to export goods and capital to sustain some politically potent industry, or the dependence of the health of the economy on raw materials imports. Less debatable than whether militarism and global adventures are unavoidable for the economic needs of capitalism per se is the historical fact that American men of power invariably are ready to embark on a major role in one or more regions, and this propensity leads to material or social consequences and conflicts with other capitalist nations no less distinctive and repetitive than inexorable economic compulsions. Spending on arms and their use, which provides short-term prosperity, over the long run creates conditions that can accelerate the system's decline.

Even if one could show that the dependence of American capitalism on the world economy and resources was not essential to general domestic prosperity—a proposition increasingly less tenable each year—the fact remains that the political influence of those corporations with most to gain overseas has always been greatly disproportionate to their numbers. Not only have they created a larger consensus among other power constituencies regarding the desirable role of the United States in the world, but they have provided, to a remarkable extent, the personnel and expertise essential for the evaluation and direction of foreign policy.

Today, even as the main capitalist nations continue their unanimity against genuine social revolution in the Third World, they are once again developing very profound economic contradictions, which they merely evade without resolving. The international trade and monetary crisis, growing rivalries for oil and other critical raw materials, and the desire to integrate the same excolonial areas into opposing spheres of economic influence, now define the escalating power conflict between Western Europe, Japan, and the United States. Whether militarism and atavistic nationalism will once more accompany these conflicts is less sure than the certainty that yet again relations between powerful capitalist states are deteriorating seriously. War in Vietnam has made the new assertiveness and real power of other nations possible, as the inflation- and deficit-ridden American economy since 1967 has barely managed to skirt the edge of a profound crisis.

In the end, all that American capitalism makes certain is uncertainty itself, presenting only a future of many and frequent crises. If radical critics cannot predict a timetable or the exact magnitude of future difficulties, men of power have never offered viable and durable means for avoiding them. But for those who rule our political and economic institutions, the challenges are theirs to inherit and resolve, and their past incapacity to do so without generating turmoil for the rest of American society and war for hapless Third World nations bequeaths us all with a dismal future.

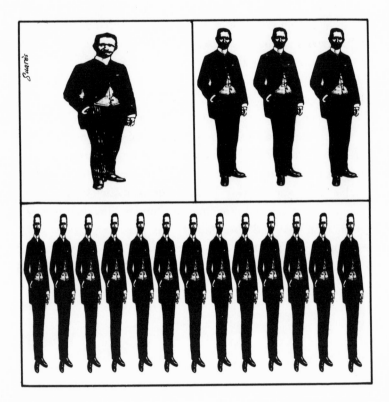

JOHN KENNETH GALBRAITH
Power and the Useful Economist

Despite all temptations to belong to other professions, John Kenneth Galbraith remains an economist. In the following essay—his 1972 presidential address to the American Economic Association—Galbraith considers the faults of contemporary "mainstream" economics. Its most serious deficiency, in his view, is that it has no useful handle for grasping the most critical problems that beset modern society: enormously costly preparation for war, which leads to trigger-happiness, extreme economic inequality, which leads to extreme social tensions, and the uglification of the civic and natural environment, which leads to the debasement of man, woman, and child.

By slurring over the role of power in the economy, Galbraith holds, economics destroys its relationship with the real world, and (perhaps unwittingly) becomes fancy apologetics for capitalism as it is. By facing up to the reality of power, by observing the inadequate or poor social performance of even that part of the economy that is competitive, economists may emancipate themselves from the follies of current economic belief and contribute to the emancipation of the state from what Galbraith calls "the planning system," by which he essentially means the power-laden large corporations.

In the past the essence of American business power, in my view, has been not so much conspiratorial as ideological; that is, it has provided the value conceptions and goals and set the limits upon what the nation is doing or trying to do. Those conceptions must now be made more humane and sensitive to the needs and aspirations of

all people, but especially of those at the bottom of society. The ideo-
logical limits that have prevented us from using our matchless re-
sources of energy and imagination for improving the conditions of
society need to be widened and deepened.

I

The ceremonial address of the president of the American Economic Association is an art form which, I imagine like most of
my predecessors, I have thoughtfully reviewed. On occasion, in
the past, the addresses have dealt with some substantive problem
of our subject or some afflicting problem of the economy. More
often they have dealt, always a shade critically, with the method-
ology of economics. While the larger science has been accepted,
there has been adverse comment on the detailed elements of its
practice. Economics is insufficiently normative. Model-building
has become an end, not a means. For several recent years in suc-
cession the criticism—which involved a certain element of personal introspection—included an exceptionally grave attack on
mathematical economics. The style of these addresses, I might
note in passing, is as distinctive as the subject matter. It features
the thoughtful solemnity of men who sense that we are speaking
for the ages. It may be worth a moment's time, on these great oc-
casions, to recall that ours is a subject which features defeated expectations.

I am moved to depart from the established rites. I should like
to concern myself with basic questions of assumption and structure. If this breaks with tradition, it does not break with present
professional tendency. We meet at a time when criticism is general, when the larger body of established theory is under exten-

sive attack. Within the last half-dozen years what before was simply called "economics" in the nonsocialist world has come to be designated "neoclassical economics," with appropriate overtures to the Keynesian and post-Keynesian development. From being a general and accepted theory of economic behavior this has become a special and debatable interpretation of such behavior. For a new and notably articulate generation of economists a reference to neoclassical economics has become markedly pejorative.

I would judge as well as hope that the present attack will prove decisive. The established theory has reserves of strength. It sustains much minor refinement, which does not raise the question of overall validity or usefulness. It survives strongly in the textbooks, although even in this stronghold one senses anxiety among the more progressive or commercially sensitive authors. Perhaps there are limits to what the young will accept.

And the arrangements by which orthodoxy is conserved in the modern academy also remain formidable. In its first half-century or so as a subject of instruction and research economics was subject to censorship by outsiders. Businessmen and their political and ideological acolytes kept watch on departments of economics and reacted promptly to heresy, the latter being anything that seemed to threaten the sanctity of property, profits, a proper tariff policy, or a balanced budget, or which involved sympathy for unions, public ownership, public regulation or, in any organized way, the poor. The growing power and self-confidence of the educational estate, the formidable and growing complexity of our subject and, no doubt, the increasing acceptability of our ideas has largely relieved us of this intervention. In leading centers of instruction faculty responsibility is either secure or increasingly so. But in place of the old censorship has come a new despotism. That consists in defining scientific excellence as whatever is closest in belief and method to the scholarly tendency of the people who are already there. This is a pervasive and oppressive thing, not the less dangerous for being, in the frequent case, both self-righteous and unconscious.

But there are problems even with this control. Neoclassical or neo-Keynesian economics, though providing unlimited opportunity for demanding refinement, has a decisive flaw. It offers no useful handle for grasping the economic problems that now beset the modern society. And these problems are obtrusive: they will not lie down and die as a favor to our profession. No arrangement for the perpetuation of thought is secure if that thought does not make contact with the problems it is presumed to solve.

I will not omit to mention the failures of neoclassical theory. But I want also to urge the means by which we can reassociate ourselves with reality. Some of this will summarize past argument; more is in a book that is to be published. At this stage even the most conservative among my listeners will be reassured. To speak well of one's own published and unpublished writing, whatever one's other aberrations, is strongly in our professional tradition.

II

The most commonplace features of neoclassical and neo-Keynesian economics are the assumptions by which power, and therewith political content, is removed from the subject. The business firm is subordinate to the instruction of the market and, thereby, to the individual or household. The state is subordinate to the instruction of the citizen. There are exceptions, but these are to the general and controlling rule, and it is firmly on the rule that neoclassical theory is positioned. If the business firm is subordinate to the market—if that is its master—then it does not have power to deploy in the economy save as this is in the service of the market and the consumer. And the winning of action to influence or rig the behavior of markets apart, it cannot bring power to bear on the state, for there the citizen is in charge.

The decisive weakness in neoclassical and neo-Keynesian economics is not the error in the assumptions by which it elides the problem of power. The capacity for erroneous belief is very great, especially where it coincides with convenience. Rather in eliding power—in making economics a nonpolitical subject—neoclassical theory, by the same process, destroys its relation with the real world. The problems of this world, moreover, are increasing both in their number and in the depth of their social affliction. In consequence neoclassical and neo-Keynesian economics is relegating its players to the social sidelines, where they either call no plays or urge the wrong ones.

Specifically, the exclusion of power and the resulting political content from economics causes it to foretell only two intrinsic and important economic problems. One of these is the microeconomic problem of market imperfection—more specifically, of monopoly or oligopoly in product or factor markets—leading to aberration in resource and income distribution. The other is the macroeconomic problem of unemployment or inflation—of a deficiency or excess in the aggregate demand for goods and services, including that associated with monetary effects. And on both problems the failure is dramatic. Neoclassical economics leads to the wrong solution of the microeconomic problem and to no solution of the macroeconomic problem. Meanwhile it leaves a whole galaxy of other urgent economic issues largely untouched.

It is now the considered sense of the community, even of econ-

139

omists when unhampered by professional doctrine, that the most prominent areas of market oligopoly—automobiles, rubber, chemicals, plastics, alcohol, tobacco, detergents, cosmetics, computers, bogus health remedies, space adventure—are areas, not of low but of high development, not of inadequate but of excessive resource use. And there is a powerful instinct that in some areas of monopoly or oligopoly, most notably in the production of weapons and weapons systems, resource use is dangerously vast.

In further contradiction of the established microeconomic conclusions we have an increasing reaction by the community to deficient resource use in industries that, at least in the scale and structure of the firm, approach the market model. Housing, health services, and local transportation are among the leading cases. The deprivation and social distress that follow from the poor performance of these industries are also something that, in their nondoctrinal manifestation, most economists take for granted.

The defender of the established doctrine does, of course, argue that excess and deprivation in resource use in the areas just mentioned reflect consumer choice. And in the areas of deprivation he can rightly insist that the fault lies with firms that, though small, are local monopolies or reflect the monopoly power of unions. These explanations beg two remarkably obvious questions: Why does the modern consumer increasingly tend to insanity, increasingly insist on self-abuse? And why do little monopolies perform badly and the big ones too well?

In fact, the neoclassical model has no explanation of the most important microeconomic problem of our time. That problem is why we have a highly unequal development, as between industries of great market power and industries of slight market power, with the development, in defiance of all doctrine, greatly favoring the first.[1]

The macroeconomic failure has been, if anything, more embarrassing. Save in its strictly mystical manifestation in one branch of monetary theory, modern macroeconomic policy depends for its validity and workability on the neoclassical market. That market, whether competitive, monopolistic, or oligopolistic, is the ultimate and authoritative instruction to the profit-maximizing firm. When output and employment are deficient, policy requires that aggregate demand be increased; this is an instruction to the market to which firms in turn respond. When the economy is at or near the effective capacity of the plant and the labor force, and inflation is the relevant social discomfort, the remedy is reversed. Demand is curtailed; the result is either an initial effect on prices or a delayed one as surplus labor seeks employment, interest rates fall, and lower factor costs bring stable or lower prices.

Such is the accepted basis of policy. It follows faithfully from the neoclassical faith in the market. The practical consequences of pursuing it need no elucidation. It has been tried in recent years in every developed country. The common result has been politically unacceptable unemployment, persistent and (in my view) socially damaging inflation or, more often, a combination of the two. The extreme failure has been, not surprisingly, in the most advanced industrial country, the United States. But the recent experience of Britain has been almost equally disenchanting.

[1] It will· be observed that performance in agriculture, an industry in which the firm has little market power, is not adverse. But it should also be observed that in no industry has power over prices been more completely removed to public authority or is there greater effort at collective control.

141

One gathers that there may be Canadian politicians who now believe that a combination of unemployment and inflation is not the best platform on which to fight a general election.

We should not deny ourselves either the instruction or the amusement that comes from the recent history of the United States in this matter. Four years ago Mr. Nixon came to office with a firm commitment to neoclassical orthodoxy. In this he was supported by some of its most distinguished and devout exponents in all the land. His subsequent discovery that he was a Keynesian involved no precipitate or radical departure from this faith. The discovery came thirty-five years after *The General Theory;* as I have just noted, all neo-Keynesian policy rests firmly on the paramount role of the market. But then a year and a half ago, facing reelection, he found that his economists' commitment to neoclassical and Keynesian orthodoxy, however admirable in the abstract, was a luxury that he could no longer afford. He apostatized to wage and price control; so, with exemplary flexibility of mind, did his economists, although admittedly this acceptance of the real world has still to survive its critical test, which is the apostates' return to computers and classrooms. But our admiration for this pliability should not keep us from recalling that, when the President changed course, no American economists were anywhere working on the policy he was forced by circumstances to adopt. And it is even more disturbing that few are now working on the policy we have been forced to follow.

More economists, in fact, are still concerning themselves with the effort to reconcile controls with the neoclassical market. This has involved an unrewarding combination of economics and archeology with wishful thinking. It holds that an inflationary momentum developed during the late nineteen-sixties in connection with the financing, or underfinancing, of the Vietnam war. And inflationary expectations became part of business and trade-union calculation. The momentum and expectation still survive. The controls are necessary until these are dissipated. Then the neoclassical and neo-Keynesian world will return, along with the appropriate policies, in all their quiet comfort. We may be sure that will not happen. Nor will we expect it to happen, if we see the role of power and political decision in modern economic behavior.

III

In place of the market system, we must now assume that for approximately half of all economic output there is a power, or planning, system (the latter term seems to me more descriptive, less pejorative, and thus preferable). The planning system consists in the United States of, at the most, two thousand large corporations. In their operation they have power that transcends the market. They rival, where they do not borrow from, the power of the state. My views on these matters will be familiar at least to some, and I shall spare myself the pleasure of extensive repetition. I cannot think that the power of the modern corporation, the purposes for which it is used, or the associated power of the modern union would seem implausible or even very novel were they not in conflict with the vested doctrine.

Thus we agree that the modern corporation, either by itself or in conjunction with others, has extensive influence over its prices and its major costs. Can we doubt that it goes beyond its prices and the market to persuade its customers? Or that it goes back of its costs to organize supply? Or that from its earnings or the

143

possession of financial affiliates it seeks to control its sources of capital? Or that its persuasion of the consumer joined with the similar effort of other firms—and with the more than incidental blessing of neoclassical pedagogy—helps establish the values of the community, notably the association between well-being and the progressively increased consumption of the products of this part of the economy?

And as citizens, if not as scholars, we would not deny that the modern corporation has a compelling position in the modern state. What it needs in research and development, technically qualified people, public works, emergency financial support, becomes public policy. So does the military procurement that sustains the demand for numerous of its products. So, perhaps, does the foreign policy that justifies the military procurement. And the means by which this power is brought to bear on the state is widely accepted. It requires an organization to deal with an organization. And between public and private bureaucracies—between General Motors and the Department of Transportation, General Dynamics and the Pentagon—there is a deeply symbiotic relationship. Each of these organizations can do much for the other. There is even, between them, a large and continuous interchange of executive personnel.

Finally, over this exercise of power and much enhancing it is the rich gloss of reputability. The men who guide the modern corporation, including the financial, legal, technical, advertising, and other sacerdotal authorities in corporate function, are the most respectable, affluent, and prestigious members of the national community. They are the Establishment. Their interest tends to become the public interest. It is an interest that even some economists find it comfortable and rewarding to avow.

That interest, needless to say, is profoundly concerned with power—with winning acceptance by others of the collective or corporate purpose. It does not disavow profits. These are important for ensuring the autonomy of the management—what I have called the technostructure—and for bringing the supply of capital within the control of the firm. Profits are also a source of prestige and therewith of influence. But of paramount importance is the much more directly political goal of growth. Such growth carries a strong economic reward; it directly enhances the pay, perquisites, and opportunities for promotion of the members of the technostructure. And it consolidates and enhances authority. It does this for the individual—for the man who now heads a larger organization or a larger part of an organization than before. And it increases the influence of the corporation as a whole.

Neoclassical economics is not without an instinct for survival. It rightly sees the unmanaged sovereignty of the consumer, the ultimate sovereignty of the citizen, and the maximization of profits and resulting subordination of the firm to the market, as the three legs of a tripod on which it stands. These are what exclude the role of power in the system. All three propositions tax the capacity for belief. That the modern consumer is the object of a massive management effort by the producer is not readily denied. The methods of such management, by their nature, are embarrassingly visible. It can only be argued that somehow it all cancels out. Elections in the United States and Canada are now being fought on the issue of the subordination of the state to corporate interest. As voters, economists accept the validity of the issue. Only their teaching denies it. But the commitment of the modern corporate bureaucracy to its expansion is, perhaps, the clearest of all. That the modern conglomerate always pursues profit over aggrandizement is believed by none. It is a common-

145

place of these last years, strongly reflected in securities' prices, that agglomeration has always been good for growth but often bad for earnings.

There remains in the modern economy—and this I stress—a world of small firms where the instruction of the market is still paramount, where costs are given, where the state is remote and subject through the legislature to the traditional pressures of economic-interest groups, and where profit maximization alone is consistent with survival. We should not think of this as the classically competitive part of the system—in contrast with the monopolistic or oligopolistic sector from which the planning system has evolved. Rather, in its combination of competitive and monopolistic structures, it approaches the entire neoclassical model. We have, to repeat, two systems. In one, power is still, as ever, contained by the market. In another and still evolving system, power extends incompletely but comprehensively to markets, to the people who patronize them, to the state and thus, ultimately, to resource use. The coexistence of these two systems becomes, in turn, a major clue to economic performance.

IV

Power being so comprehensively deployed in a very large part of the total economy, there can no longer, except for reasons of game-playing or more deliberate intellectual evasion, be any separation by economists between economics and politics. When the modern corporation acquires power over markets, power in the community, power over the state, power over belief, it is a political instrument, different in form and degree but not in kind from the state itself. To hold otherwise—to deny the political character of the modern corporation—is not merely to avoid the reality. It is to disguise the reality. The victims of that disguise are those we instruct in error. The beneficiaries are the institutions whose power we so disguise. Let there be no question: economics, so long as it is thus taught, becomes, however unconsciously, a part of an arrangement by which the citizen or student is kept from seeing how he is, or will be, governed.

This does not mean that economics now becomes a branch of political science. That is a prospect by which we would rightly be repelled. Political science is also the captive of its stereotypes—including that of citizen control of the state. Also, while economics cherishes thought, at least in principle, political science regularly accords reverence to the man who knows only what has been done before. Economics does not become a part of political science. But politics does—and must—become a part of economics.

There will be fear that once we abandon present theory, with its intellectually demanding refinement and its increasing instinct for measurement, we shall lose the filter by which scholars are separated from charlatans and windbags. The latter are always a danger, but there is more danger in remaining with a world that is not real. And we shall be surprised, I think, at the new clarity and intellectual consistency with which we see our world, once power is made a part of our system. To such a view let me now turn.

V

In the neoclassical view of the economy a general identity of interest between the goals of the business firm and those of the community could be assumed. The firm was subject to the instruction of the community, either through the market or the ballot box. People could not be fundamentally in conflict with themselves—always given some reasonable decency in income distribution. Once the firm in the planning system is seen to have comprehensive power to pursue its own interest, this assumption becomes untenable. Perhaps by accident its interests are those of the public, but there is no organic reason why this must be so. In the absence of proof to the contrary, divergence of interest, not identity of interest, must be assumed.

The nature of the conflict also becomes predictable. Growth being a principal goal of the planning system, it will be great where power is great. And in the market sector of the economy growth will, at least by comparison, be deficient. This will not, as neoclassical doctrine holds, be because people have an amiable tendency to misunderstand their needs. It will be because the system is so constructed as to serve badly their needs and then to win greater or less acquiescence in the result. That the present system should lead to an excessive output of automobiles, an improbable effort to cover the economically developed sections of the planet with asphalt, a lunar preoccupation with moon exploration, a fantastically expensive and potentially suicidal investment in missiles, submarines, bombers, and aircraft carriers, is as one would expect. These are the industries with power to command resources for growth. And central to public purpose—to sound resource utilization—will be a cutback in such industries, as all instinct now suggests. Thus does the introduction of power ·as a comprehensive aspect of our system correct present error. Let us not fail to note that these are exactly the industries in which an uncomplicated neoclassical view of monopoly and oligopoly and of profit maximization at the expense of ideal resource use would, of all things, suggest an expansion of output. How wrong are we allowed to be!

The counterpart of excessive resource use in the planning system where power is comprehensively deployed is a relatively deficient resource use where power is circumscribed. Such will be the case in the part of the economy where competition and entrepreneurial monopoly, as distinct from great organization, are the rule. And if the product or service is closely related to comfort or survival, the discontent will be considerable. That housing, health services, local transportation, some household services, are now areas of grave inadequacy is agreed. It is in such industries that all modern governments seek to expand resource use. Here, in desperation, even the devout free-enterprisers accept the need of social action, even of socialism.

Again, we may observe, the error of economics is prejudicial. Although as citizens we advocate restraint in the area of excessive resource use, our teaching does not. And though as citizens we urge social action where the firm approaches the neoclassical norm, our teaching does not. In the latter case we not only disguise corporate power, but we make remedial action in such areas as housing, health care, and transportation also abnormal— the consequence of sui generis error that is never quite explained. This is unfortunate, for here are tasks that require imagination, pride, and determination.

VI

When power is admitted to our calculus, our macroeconomic embarrassment also disappears. Economics makes plausible what governments are forced, in practice, to do. Corporations have power in their markets. So, and partly in consequence, do unions. The competitive claims of unions can most conveniently be resolved by passing the cost of settlement along to the public. Measures to arrest this exercise of power by limiting aggregate demand must be severe. And, not surprisingly, the power of the planning system has been brought to bear to exclude those macroeconomic measures that have a primary effect on that system. Thus monetary policy is entirely permissible; that is at least partly because its primary effect is on the neoclassical entrepreneur who must borrow money. Monetary constraint is far less painful for the large established corporation which, as an elementary exercise of power, has ensured itself a supply of capital from earnings or financial affiliates or morally affiliated banks. The power of the planning system in the community has also won immunity for public expenditures important to itself: highways, industrial research, rescue loans, national defense. These have the sanction of a higher public purpose. A similar, if still slightly less successful, effort is being made on behalf of corporate and personal taxes. So fiscal policy has also been accommodated to the interests of the planning system.

Thus the inevitability of controls. The interaction of corporate and trade-union power can be made to yield only to the strongest fiscal and monetary restraints. Those restraints that are available have a comparatively benign effect on those with power, but they weigh adversely on people who vote. When no election is in prospect, perhaps such a policy is possible. It will earn applause for its respectability. But it cannot be tolerated by anyone who must weigh its popular effect.

As with the need for social action and organization in the market sector, there are many reasons why it would be well were economists to accept the inevitability of wage and price control. It would help keep politicians, responding to the resonance of their own past instruction, from supposing controls to be wicked and unnatural, and hence temporary, to be abandoned whenever they seemed to be working. This is a poor mood in which to develop sound administration. And it would cause economists themselves to consider how controls can be made workable and how the effect on income distribution can be made equitable. With controls this last becomes a serious matter. The market is no longer a disguise for inequality, however egregious, in income distribution. Much inequality must be seen to be the result of relative power.

VII

When power is made part of our system, yet other matters of considerable current moment are illuminated. Thus the counterpart of systemic differences in development, as between the planning and market sectors of the economy, is systemic sectoral differences in income. In the neoclassical system resource mobility is assumed, broadly speaking, to equalize interindustry return. If there is inequality, it is the result of barriers to movement. Now we see that, given its comprehensive market power, the planning system can protect itself from adverse movements in its terms of trade. The same power allows it to accept unions, for it need not absorb even temporarily their demands. In the market system—some areas of monopoly or union power apart—there is no similar control of the terms of trade. Given the absence of market power, there can be no similar yielding on wage costs, for there is no similar certainty that they can be passed on. (It is because of the

151

character of the industry he seeks to organize, not his original power, that Cesar Chavez is for so many the new Lenin.) And in the market system the self-employed have the option—not present in the planning system—of reducing their own wages (and sometimes those of families or immediate employees) in order to survive.

Thus there is a built-in inequality in income between the two systems. And thus also the case for minimum-wage legislation, support to trade unions in agriculture, price-support legislation, and most important, perhaps, a floor under family income, as antidotes to such interindustry inequality. Again this view of matters fits our present concerns. Minimum-wage legislation, price-support legislation, and support to collective bargaining are all questions of continuing political controversy as they apply to small business and agriculture. They are not serious issues in highly organized industry—in the planning system. And the question of a floor under family income, a matter of intense political argument, has recently divided those workers in the planning system who would not be beneficiaries from those in the market system who would be. Again there is reassurance in a view of the economy that prepares us for the politics of our time.

The inclusion of power in economic calculus also prepares us for the great debate over the environment. It is the claim of neoclassical economics that it foresaw possible environmental consequences from economic development—that it, some time ago, embraced the concept of external diseconomies of production and, by inference, of consumption. Alas, this is a modest claim. The noninclusion of external diseconomies was long viewed as a minor defect of the price system, an afterthought for an hour's classroom discussion. And, as E. J. Mishan has observed, it was largely ignored in the textbooks. Nor does the notion of external diseconomies now offer a useful remedy. No one can suppose, or really supposes, that more than a fraction of the damage—especially that to the beauty and tranquility of our surroundings—could be compensated in any useful way by internalizing external diseconomies.

If growth is the central and rewarding purpose of the firm, and if power is comprehensively available to impose this goal on the society, the possibility of conflict between private growth and public purpose as regards the environment is immediately plausible. So, since this power depends extensively not on force but persuasion, is the effort to make pollution seem palatable or worth the cost, including the effort to make advertising of remedial action a substitute for action. And so is the remedy to which all industrial countries are being forced. This is not, primarily, to internalize external diseconomies. Rather, it is to specify the legal parameters within which growth may proceed or, as in the case of automobile use in central cities, airplane use over urban areas, the SST, industrial, commercial, and residential appropriation of countryside and roadside, the kinds of growth that are inconsistent with public purpose. We would have saved much corruption of our surroundings if our economics had held such action to be the predictable consequence of the pursuit of present economic goals and not the exceptional result of a peculiar aberration of the price system.

We had best, in any case, have the right guide to action for the future, for there is a strong conservative case for such guidance. While economists toy weakly with external diseconomies, others are arguing that growth itself is the villain. They are seeking its extinction. To see environmental damage as a natural consequence of planning power and purpose and to see, in consequence, the need for confining growth within parameters that

153

protect the public interest could be important for ensuring continued economic growth.

Finally, when power becomes part of our system, so does Ralph Nader. We are prepared for the explosion of concern now called consumerism. If the consumer is the ultimate source of authority, his abuse is an occasional fault. He cannot be fundamentally at odds with an economic system that he commands. But if the producing firm has comprehensive power and purposes of its own, there is every likelihood of conflict. Technology is then subordinate to the strategy of consumer persuasion. Products are changed, not to make them better, but to take advantage of the belief that what is new is better. There is a high failure rate in engineering, not what is better, but what can be sold. The consumer—the unpersuaded or disenchanted consumer—rebels. This is not a rebellion against minor matters of fraud or misinformation. It is a major reaction against a whole deployment of power by which the consumer is made the instrument of purposes that are not his own.

VIII

There are two conclusions to which this exercise—to which incorporation of power into our system—compels us. The first, in a way, is encouraging. It is that economists' work is not yet done. On the contrary, it is just beginning. If we accept the reality of power as part of our system, we have years of useful work ahead of us. And since we will be in touch with real issues, and since issues that are real inspire passion, our life will, again, be pleasantly contentious, perhaps even usefully dangerous.

The other conclusion concerns the state. For when we make

power and therewith politics a part of our system, we can no longer escape or disguise the contradictory character of the modern state. The state is the prime object of economic power. It is captured. Yet on all the matters I have mentioned—the restrictions on excessive resource use, organization to offset inadequate resource use, controls, action to correct systemic inequality, protection of the environment, protection of the consumer—remedial action lies with the state. The fox is powerful in the management of the coop. To this management the chickens must look for redress.

Thus perhaps our greatest question. Is emancipation of the state from the control of the planning system possible? No one knows. And in the absence of knowledge no one certainly will suggest that it will be easy. But there is a gleam of encouragement. As ever circumstances are forcing the pace.

In the United States the recent election was fought, all but exclusively, over issues in which the purposes of the planning system or its major participants diverge from those of the public. The question of defense expenditures is such an issue. That of tax reform is another. The deprivation in housing, mass transportation, health services, and city services is yet another—one that reflects the relative inability of these industries to organize and command resources. The question of a guaranteed income is another such issue. Its effect, as I have noted, is on incomes outside the planning system—on the exploited in the market system, those who are rejected by both. The environment is such an issue—with its conflict between the technostructure's goal of growth and the public's concern for its surroundings. Only wage and price control was not an issue in the recent election. That was almost certainly because economists of orthodox tendency on both sides found the prospect too embarrassing to discuss.

I do not mention these issues with any purpose save to show that the questions that emerge when power is made a part of our calculus are present and real. We need hardly remind ourselves that political issues are made not by parties and politicians but by circumstance.

Once power is made part of our system, we will not, of course, escape the political contention that comes from dealing with issues that are real. This brings me to my last point. I do not plead for partisanship in our economics but for neutrality. But let us be clear as to what is neutral. If the state must be emancipated from economic interest, a neutral economics would not deny the need. This is what economics now does. It tells the young and susceptible and the old and vulnerable that economic life has no content of power and politics because the firm is safely subordinate to the market and to the state and for this reason it is safely at the command of the consumer and citizen. Such an economics is not neutral. It is the influential and invaluable ally of those whose exercise of power depends on an acquiescent public. If the state is the executive committee of the great corporation and the planning system, it is partly because neoclassical economics is its instrument for neutralizing suspicion that this is so. I have spoken of the emancipation of the state from economic interest. For the economist there can be no doubt about where this task begins. It is with the emancipation of economic belief.

NAME INDEX